PRAISE FOR *THE M&A SOLUTION*

"Once again, Don has done a masterful job of bringing a practical, values-based approach to the forefront of the corporate consciousness. As we see the predicted new cycle of M&A activity start ramping up, this book—and Don's wisdom—is an absolute must."

—Craig Buchholz
senior vice president, global communications, General Motors

"Don is a true M&A master. His stellar success is rooted in his dual focus on values and valuation. In this book, he deftly defines/puts structure to the often-nebulous area of company values. That's exactly what modern companies need to survive and thrive postmerger or acquisition. You will learn the value and how to apply it to your next deal."

—Fran Biderman-Gross
Don's coauthor of How to Lead a Values-Based Professional Services Firm

"*The M&A Solution: A Values-Based Approach to Integrate Companies* is a must read for anyone actively involved in mergers and acquisitions. Don's perspective—honed over thirty years of deal making—is a clarion call to buyers and sellers alike that values and purpose matter, and matter big."

—Adam Lavelle
chief solutions officer, global alliances, Dentsu

"Hands down the best read for insights into M&A! It can be an intimidating process to make deals for other companies when still trying to grow your own. But when you see there is a proven process and methodology for success, your plan becomes reality. Don Scales's new book, *The M&A Solution: A Values-Based Approach to Integrate Companies*, makes the right connections for M&A insight, expressing a professional, eye-opening set of possibilities to acquisitive growth."

—Jeff Herzog
founder and former CEO, iCrossing and ZogMedia

"With nearly forty M&A deals under his belt, Don has uncovered the key to successful M&A, and it's all about ensuring values are compatible and aligned."

—Kristen Kalupski
VP of marketing, Investis Digital

"When Don Scales offers to share what he's learned, pay attention. In *The M&A Solution: A Values-Based Approach to Integrate Companies*, Don demystifies the drivers of successful acquisitions for industry outsiders. Don has the knowledge, the experience, and the scars that we can all learn from. I highly recommend this book for anyone on the buy or sell side of transactions."

—Cliff Farrah
president and CEO, The Beacon Group; author, Growing the Top Line

"Don Scales identifies and tackles head on the number-one driver of M&A success: *values*. Don't believe for a minute that values are a fluff topic. There is no CEO that I know who is more practical, strategic, and successful than Don. *The M&A Solution: A Values-Based Approach to Integrate Companies* will become essential reading for every growth-oriented CEO!"

—Doug Fletcher
best-selling author, How Clients Buy *and* How to Win Client Business

"My company, Vertical Measures, was acquired by Investis Digital. More than two years later, both Don and I would put that deal in the 'successful' category. Don's decades of experience—coupled with a genuine humanistic approach to business, employees, and clients—made Investis Digital the perfect fit for my company. His breadth of real-world experience in mergers and acquisitions and talent for clearly articulating complex issues, make this book one I highly recommend to all business owners."

—Arnie Kuenn
founder and former CEO, Vertical Measures

"With nearly forty M&A deals under his belt, Don has mastered the art of putting values at the heart of any successful merger or acquisition."

—Dave Johnson
COO, Investis Digital; former COO, iCrossing

"I've known Don for over twenty years. During the time working together we completed over thirty mergers and acquisitions. Don's extensive knowledge of M&As gained by personal hands-on experience makes this book a must-read. Don shares his M&A knowledge for anyone either contemplating a deal or just wanting an understanding of how to successfully close and integrate an acquisition."

—Mike Jackson
former EVP and CFO, iCrossing

"Working through many deals with Don over more than twenty years I've learned that values lead the curiosity of our organization and the numbers and technology follow, because if the values we hold dear are aligned, *success will be ours to have.* Don puts forth a convincing empirical analysis of values and how they affect the success of any transaction."

—David Corchado
chief digital officer, Investis Digital; former chief technology officer, iCrossing

THE

M&A

SOLUTION

DON SCALES

THE M&A SOLUTION

A Values-Based Approach to Integrate Companies

ForbesBooks

Published by ForbesBooks, Charleston, South Carolina.
Member of Advantage Media Group.

ForbesBooks is a registered trademark, and the ForbesBooks colophon is a trademark of Forbes Media, LLC.

Printed in the United States of America.

10 9 8 7 6 5 4 3 2 1

ISBN: 978-1-95086-338-9
LCCN: 2021903186

Cover and layout design by Mary Hamilton.

This custom publication is intended to provide accurate information and the opinions of the author in regard to the subject matter covered. It is sold with the understanding that the publisher, Advantage|ForbesBooks, is not engaged in rendering legal, financial, or professional services of any kind. If legal advice or other expert assistance is required, the reader is advised to seek the services of a competent professional.

Advantage Media Group is proud to be a part of the Tree Neutral® program. Tree Neutral offsets the number of trees consumed in the production and printing of this book by taking proactive steps such as planting trees in direct proportion to the number of trees used to print books. To learn more about Tree Neutral, please visit **www.treeneutral.com**.

Since 1917, Forbes has remained steadfast in its mission to serve as the defining voice of entrepreneurial capitalism. ForbesBooks, launched in 2016 through a partnership with Advantage Media Group, furthers that aim by helping business and thought leaders bring their stories, passion, and knowledge to the forefront in custom books. Opinions expressed by ForbesBooks authors are their own. To be considered for publication, please visit **www.forbesbooks.com**.

I take great pride in the companies I've had the privilege to lead. Part of that pride comes in building long-term sustainable value through acquisitions. None of this would have been possible without the support of engaged colleagues and encouraging boards. So, thanks to you all. It has been quite a ride so far.

CONTENTS

INTRODUCTION

Mergers and acquisitions need a new playbook. You are reading it now. According to the *Harvard Business Review*, companies spend more than $2 trillion on acquisitions each year.[1] Yet research studies have found time and again that between 70 percent and 90 percent of mergers and acquisitions (M&As) fail. That 20 percent delta can be explained by the types of firms involved in each study—public, private, international, small, midsized, large, and so on—and the size of the M&A. For example, McKinsey & Company has found that the larger the deal, the more likely it is to fail.[2] Thus, if a study was focused on

---

1   Christensen, Clayton M., Richard Alton, Curtis Rising, and Andrew Waldeck. "The New M&A Playbook." *Harvard Business Review* 89, no. 3 (March 2011) https://www.hbs.edu/faculty/Pages/item.aspx?num=39920.

2   Dariush Bahreini, Roerich Bansal, Gerd Finck, and Marjan Firouzgar. "Done deal? Why many large transactions fail to cross the finish line." McKinsey & Company Strategy & Corporate Finance Practice (August 2019) https://www.mckinsey.com/business-functions/strategy-and-corporate-finance/our-insights/done-deal-why-many-large-transactions-fail-to-cross-the-finish-line.

large M&As, the failure rate was likely greater than studies focused on smaller or niche-sector M&As.

Each researcher's definition of success also plays a part. Was success based on increased market cap? Over what time frame? Was it based on achieving a set of diversification or synergy goals? Based on something else? However, no matter what metric of success was used, more than two-thirds of the deals failed to achieve their objectives.

The realization that M&As have a strong chance of failing is nothing new. For example, a survey conducted by KPMG[3] more than twenty years ago found that only 17 percent of surveyed M&A deals added value to the combined company, 30 percent had no impact, and about *53 percent actually destroyed value*. In other words, 83 percent of M&As reported by respondents were unsuccessful in producing any business benefit when shareholder value was the benchmark for success.

You would think that with the advances in data, technology, and transparency during the two decades since the KPMG study was released, we would be getting better at M&A. Yet that north-of-70-percent failure rate persists. We fill out financial checklists; we verify data; we make personal on-site visits and poke around every office, cubicle, file cabinet, and hidden cubby hole. But in the end, you have a better chance at winning at the tables in Las Vegas than putting together a successful merger or acquisition transaction and integration.

No matter what we do, a significant number of M&As fail, and a significant amount of capital is wasted. Add in the 10 percent of deals that never have a chance to fail because they are abandoned before they close,[4] and it is obvious—Houston, we have a problem.

---

3   KPMG Mergers and Acquisitions: Global Research Report 1999. "Unlocking Share-holder Value: The Keys to Success." November 1999. http://people.stern.nyu.edu/adamodar/pdfiles/eqnotes/KPMGM&A.pdf.

4   Bahreini, et al. "Done Deal?"

As a wise person once said, if what we are doing time and again results in the same failing outcome, shouldn't we be doing something different?

I have been working in the professional services business for more than thirty years. During that time I've been involved in more than forty M&A deals, on both the buyer and seller side. Most involved fully integrating the two companies. Some involved allowing the acquired entity to remain relatively independent. Some were mergers of equals. Some were acquisitions of small firms by much larger ones. Most succeeded in meeting their expected goals. Some did not. I have a much better win/loss record than the average bear, but the deals that fell apart bothered me. I don't like to lose.

When I was young, my mother used to quietly encourage me and say, "Someone has to win. There's no reason it can't be you." Well, it could only be me if I was prepared to win. If I had practiced and knew the right strategies to implement in varying game scenarios. If I lost, I made it my business to figure out why so I'd be more prepared to win next time. When I was part of a failed acquisition (or even a deal that simply wasn't as successful as I'd expected), I also made it my business to explore why. The competitive spirit encouraged by my mother kicked me into high gear. If I was going to win next time, I needed to know why I had lost this time.

While analyzing deals that fell apart—whether it involved my company or others in the news—I began to recognize a pattern. Deals floundered not because we lacked due diligence. Not because someone failed to analyze the data correctly. Not because the goals were unreachable to begin with. *They floundered because the corporate values were misaligned.*

This realization hit me like a ton of bricks. Those involved in the M&A world have been so focused on checklists and financial analysis that they have missed the elephant in the room—or the people in the company. Products, market share, geographical reach, financial stability, and all the other things on the standard acquisition checklist mean nothing if the ways the individual companies conduct their business are at odds.

I think I've always instinctively known that a company's values and corporate culture were important. But I'm not sure I realized just how important. When you are in the "infatuation" phase of an acquisition, it's easy to overlook and rationalize things that should give you pause. After all, you have stars in your eyes. You don't want to pause! You want to get on to the "happily ever after" phase. And, frankly, decision makers are usually more comfortable basing their decisions on objective bottom lines than on softer aspects of a company like "values."

Back when I was just starting in the professional services industry, companies were simply expected to provide a service to their clients in a professional manner. Customers were expected to pay in a timely manner. Profits were determined by how effectively and efficiently executives ran the firm. There was none better at explaining all this than David Maister in his seminal work, *Managing the Professional Services Firm*. This book has become the bible for those managing professional services firms.

Despite being a bit dated from a cultural standpoint—at that time, there was no cloud-based computing, no remote workers, no social media, no Millennials demanding to know why a particular process was important or how it would affect other people—the strategies outlined in this book are still very valid when it comes to management practices. However, over time, I have come to realize that there is a huge missing strategic piece: leadership, values, and culture.

Every company has a culture. Every company has a set of values. Every company has leaders. When considering an acquisition—either as the acquirer or the acquiree—you must understand the culture and values of the other company and how its leadership interacts with employees and customers. It is very possible for two successful firms—each with sound balance sheets and strong growth prospects—to have clashing cultures. In the past the cultural differences weren't considered important. If anyone even noticed misaligned values, they tended to gloss over them. Opposites attract! It will create synergy! We'll take the best practices from each company and combine them into a new and improved corporate culture 2.0!

Those clichés rarely work. Opposites might attract, but they don't often work well together. The strongest performers will often leave, taking with them the institutional knowledge and skill sets that made the company successful in the first place. Growth slows, then stops. Pretty soon, the companies are looking for an exit strategy.

The purpose of this book is to mitigate that culture-clash risk. If you can reduce that risk, you can increase the odds of succeeding. It's that simple.

The purpose of this book is to mitigate that culture-clash risk. If you can reduce that risk, you can increase the odds of succeeding. It's that simple.

Now, fitting values, culture, and leadership into a checklist isn't simple. There will be a lot of subjective guestimates going on. But it is well worth the effort because you are going to want to greatly improve the chances of being part of a successful M&A. If you want your company to grow—and what leader doesn't?—you are likely to become part of a merger or acquisition sometime in your career. It's simply the most efficient and quickest way to add market share, product lines, and capabilities. As such, it would be to your benefit to learn as much as possible about the M&A process and how you can position your company for success.

To be clear, I'm not saying that all you have to look at is a company's values to know if an acquisition and subsequent integration will succeed. In order to complete a successful M&A deal, you of course must focus on the key financial and growth aspects of an acquisition outlined in Maister's book, just as you always have. And there will always be curveballs that knock you back. As I write this book, we are in the middle of the COVID-19 pandemic (at least I hope it is the middle and not still the beginning). I am also in the middle of selling a company. We were ready to advance the process when the world came screeching to a halt. The sale is now on pause as we all evaluate the impact the new economic reality will have on growth and valuations. Those things happen. Some risks are uncontrollable. But values-risk isn't one of them.

To mitigate values-risk, we need to add a new section to your checklist—a Values Compatibility Profile based on a values survey. Believe me, this is not fluff. I don't do fluff. I have a BS and an MS in chemical engineering from Rice University, as well as an MBA from the Harvard Business School. My mind deals in practicalities and realities. The processes I present in this book will be practical and actionable.

Although my background is in the professional services industry, the framework I'm going to present can be applied to any industry. A number of the basic processes will mirror those found in the Maister book because they would be hard to improve. But throughout I'm going to explain the importance of knowing your own company's values and culture and how it will impact future M&A transactions, as well as how to lead your team during and after the acquisition process. You will learn how to take the time up front to understand values—on your side and the other side—and make sure before you go further that there's a real meeting of the minds, not simply aspirational hopes. In short, you will learn how to establish solid values and culture before, during, and after the acquisition process and thus greatly improve the odds of achieving one of the relatively few successful M&As.

The next two chapters will explain when and why you would want to be part of an M&A transaction to begin with, given the long odds of success, as well as diving into why M&As fail. Then I'll move into the three parts of any M&A:

- Part I: Prepare Both Companies to Close the Deal

- Part II: The Thick of It

- Part III: Value That Will Last

When you finish the book, you will not only have a deeper understanding of why M&As need to be values-based and why you ignore values at your own peril, but I'll have also supplied you with checklists and audit templates to guide you through the process. I expect this book will be one you keep on your bookshelf next to your go-to management reference book, whether Maister's or someone else's, because it will add the missing values piece. It is, after all, designed to improve your own success.

CHAPTER ONE

WHY M&A?

After reading the introduction, you might be asking yourself why anyone in their right mind would want to be part of an M&A deal. After all, the odds of success are pretty sobering. Statistics, however, don't tell the whole story. The failure rate doesn't prove that M&As in and of themselves are prone to failure. It simply proves that *badly conceived and executed* M&As are prone to failure. The odds of success can be greatly improved if the participants slow down and take the time to survey not only the financial aspects of the deal but also the values both entities bring to the table. It might make the process a bit longer, but the benefits of a well-executed acquisition are well worth the extra effort.

For example, within twelve months of my joining iCrossing, we began to look for appropriate acquisition targets. iCrossing was one of the largest digital marketers in the United States, but I thought we had the ability to be much larger, as well as be a global player. The quickest way to reach that goal was through acquisitions. During the next few years, we quickly added capability, product lines, market share, and global reach through acquisitions. All in all, we increased revenues over 600 percent in just two years. There is no way iCrossing would have reached that size in that time frame via organic growth.

BENEFITS OF A MERGER OR ACQUISITION

There are many good reasons for growing your business through an acquisition or merger, but most boil down to accelerating the growth of your company by acquiring additional skilled personnel, assets, capabilities, and/or market share. We typically think about these benefits in terms of the acquiring firm, but in a good acquisition, the firm being acquired gains just as much as the buyer. The most successful mergers or acquisitions are a win-win for everyone involved. Some of the more common benefits that achieve those wins include:

Decreased Barriers to Entry

One of the quickest ways to enter a new market or add a new product line is to buy a firm already operating in that market or successfully producing the desired product line. Market entry is typically very costly due to the costs of market research, development of new products specific to that market, and the time needed to build a profitable client base. Through an acquisition, however, a company can instantaneously move from being a local player to a regional player, or from a national powerhouse to an international powerhouse. In the iCrossing/Spannerworks acquisition outlined in the case study box, iCrossing was quickly able to enter the UK and, eventually, continental Europe. In fact, on the day the press release went out announcing the closing of the acquisition deal, iCrossing had already changed its website and "About" statement to note "iCrossing is headquartered in Scottsdale, with offices in Atlanta, Chicago, Dallas, New York, San Francisco, and Brighton, UK." The minute the paperwork was signed, iCrossing became an international company.

Increased Market Share

Every company battles its peers for market share. Instead of slowly building your client base, it sometimes makes sense to simply acquire one or more of your rivals. A good example of this type of acquisition is Sirius Satellite Radio's acquisition of XM Satellite Radio in 2008. The new entity became the dominant player in the market—in fact, it is pretty much the only player in the market—and has remained so for the past decade. The merger of the National Football League and American Football League back in the 1960s is an example of two entities who merged primarily because the marketplace could not support two leagues with the same offerings, so both were suffering. Rather than both leagues battling for part of a limited pie, it was a win for both when they merged, and one league was able to have the entire pie.

New Competencies and Resources

Instead of doing its own in-house research and development, a company can choose to take over other businesses to gain additional competencies and resources. Facebook's $1 billion acquisition of Instagram fits this category. The social media giant was able to quickly add photo-sharing capabilities that had been developed by the stand-alone app, which complemented its own core competencies. At the time Instagram only had thirteen employees and no revenues, but its user base was growing exponentially. Today it has turned out to be one of Facebook's most profitable acquisitions.

Acquiring Assets at Less Cost than Developing Them

Companies often find that it is easier to acquire performing assets than develop them. These assets can be anything from factories and buildings to patents and equipment. For example, when Charter Communications acquired Time Warner Cable, the communications company not only inherited Time Warner's customers, but it also took over the company's cable line infrastructure and network. Building out a national network from scratch is prohibitively expensive, as well as time consuming. Buying a company with a network infrastructure in place seems like a good deal—even when the price is $78.7 billion.

Increased Access to Experts, Capital, and New Ideas

When small businesses join with larger businesses, they are typically able to access professionals, such as financial, legal, or human resource specialists, who were unavailable before. Conversely, larger firms often find the specialist knowledge of niche firms to be accretive to their own competencies. For example, Google acquired a small company, North, which makes smart glasses to use in augmented reality. Google had developed its own smart glasses in 2012, but they never took off. With the purchase of North, it is back in the sector. Acquisitions often inject new blood and energy into the business, which in turn boosts the new entity's growth.

From North's perspective, the deal gives it almost unlimited funding to continue its research, as well as a parent that can provide an instant market. In addition, although this was not at issue in the Google example, the single entity that results from an M&A integration often finds it easier to raise investment capital and financing compared to the individual efforts of the merged firms simply because size matters.

This list is not exhaustive, but it gives you an idea of why companies would take the risk on a merger or acquisition despite the long odds. In addition, these benefits are not discrete or in individual silos. There is almost always more than one reason to acquire another company. In the Facebook/Instagram example above, Facebook was able to neutralize a rising rival, in addition to capturing its technology. It was also able to increase market share in a younger demographic and gain a reputation as a company that recognized talent and was willing to pay for it.

M&AS COME IN SEVERAL FLAVORS

In addition to a variety of M&A benefits, there are a variety of business combinations or structures that can be used to describe a particular acquisition. Choosing the correct structure can be as important to the success of your venture as choosing the right partner.

Conglomerate

We typically think of acquisitions and mergers as being deals between companies with similar capabilities, markets, or product lines, but that is not always the situation. In the case of conglomerate acquisitions, the firms are involved in totally unrelated business activities. Amazon's purchase of Whole Foods in 2019 is a good example of a conglomerate M&A. Although they are both retailers, they were in completely different segments of the retail market. The purchase gave Amazon access to a national brick-and-mortar footprint, as well as entry into the growing specialty food market. Over time, a conglomerate M&A can grow into a wildly diverse company. Samsung, for example, is known for its electronics, but it is also involved in military hardware, apartments, healthcare, and even theme parks.

Horizontal Merger

A horizontal merger involves two companies in the same industry. Typically, the participants are looking to achieve cost efficiencies by eliminating redundant operations, as well as quickly reducing competition for market share. The Sirius and XM acquisition mentioned earlier was a horizontal merger. The merger of the National Football League with the American Football League was also a horizontal merger.

Market-Extension Mergers

A market-extension merger involves companies that have the same products but in separate markets. The main purpose of the market-extension merger is to give the merging companies access to each other's market, thus ensuring a bigger market universe and client base. A good example of a market-extension merger would be the acquisition of San Francisco–headquartered BankAmerica by Charlotte, NC–headquartered NationsBank. The resulting bank, Bank of America, was the largest bank in the country at the time.

Product-Extension Acquisition

A product-extension merger or acquisition takes place between two companies in the same market that deal in related products. The products don't have to be the same—they often aren't—but there needs to be a synergy that occurs when the products are combined under one roof. For example, in 2002, online auction site eBay purchased online payment site PayPal to make transactions between buyers and sellers faster and easier. Both companies benefited from the symbiotic partnership.

Vertical Merger

A vertical merger occurs when firms operating at different levels within an industry's supply chain merge operations. Most often the logic behind the acquisition is to increase synergies by merging firms that would be more efficient operating as one. The Walt Disney Company might have started life as a small animation studio, but after decades of acquisitions, it is now one of the most vertically integrated companies in the world. It owns the companies that create and produce film and television properties, which are then marketed and distributed by Disney throughout the world. The home videos are manufactured by Buena Vista Home Video, which is owned by Disney, and oftentimes shipped to Disney retail stores along with significant forms of other consumer products. Many of these toys, games, and logo wear are found in Disney's hotel, restaurants, and theme parks.

As with the benefits-of-mergers-and-acquisitions list, the merger structures aren't black and white. Conglomerate mergers can also be vertical or horizontal mergers. A horizontal merger might also add products, so it brings in aspects of a product-extension merger. But having some idea of how mergers and acquisitions are generally categorized will give you an idea of what benefits the firms are trying to achieve.

DECISION TIME

Now that we've done a quick overview of why you might want to be part of a merger or acquisition, we are down to the question: Should you?

In some cases, you don't have a choice. A private company that is large enough to buy another firm will usually have private equity investors who expect a specific return on their investment. They are not normally interested in waiting for organic growth, which can take several years, to provide this return.

Smaller or start-up private firms also often have investors anxious to cash out or at least realize a significant return on investment. Allowing itself to be acquired provides capital to such firms to buy out investors who want to leave, as well as resources to boost growth.

A public firm also needs to keep growing to satisfy the equities markets, which bake in a certain growth profile. Public firms are usually expected to show growth on a quarterly basis. Long-term research and development plans are no longer favored by the majority of impatient investors. A firm that fails to reach growth expectations will soon find itself in a downward spiral on the stock exchange. Acquiring other firms can quickly provide the growth needed to satisfy the markets and private investors.

So, outside influences (i.e., investors who expect a quick return) can play a significant role in deciding whether to pursue an acquisition strategy or wait for organic growth to build out the company.

In general, you will want to consider going the acquisition route if your business plan calls for growth and expansion within a time period that doesn't make organic growth feasible or if you simply don't have the resources to fulfill the plan without acquiring another company. It's a little hard to develop hard-and-fast criteria that result in a flashing signal indicating "Now is the time to do an acquisition!" But you'll know it's time when it becomes obvious that a merger or acquisition is the best and most efficient way to reach your business goals.

FINDING THE RIGHT COMPANY

Buying the right company takes a lot of work up front. You need to know why you are buying it. You need to know what it will bring to your firm. You need to know that your values are compatible. And you need to know that a company that does all of that exists to begin with.

When I am looking for a suitable acquisition, I first narrow down what capabilities or gaps we are looking to fill. I always buy on capabilities. In other words, I won't buy a company in Buenos Aires just because it's in Buenos Aires, even if we are looking to expand into the South American market. It does no good to chase the shiniest object or the flavor of the month. Nor is "getting a good deal" the key to success. Know what you need, and let that guide your decisions. From experience, I know the types of companies that make good acquisitions. Once I find one I like, there's a good chance that I'll acquire it.

Once we zero in on the capabilities or new business line we want to add, we might go through more than one hundred companies looking for those that are the right size, are in the right location, and have the right products. Once we have ten or so good prospects, we take a cursory look at the financials to narrow the pool down to six or seven. At that point I step in to meet with the founders, CEOs, and exec teams. This is when we begin to investigate the values and culture. Do they match ours? Are they complementary if not a match? It is only after we've found one or two with compatible values that we engage the attorneys and financial people to do their deep-dive due diligence.

Most companies are not continually in acquisition mode—but good companies and good CEOs are ready if and when the opportunity to acquire another company presents itself. It is part of a CEO's job to understand what's in the marketplace, what companies are out there, and which ones could add some value.

One of the easiest ways to be ready to proceed with an acquisition if one is needed—and find those one hundred companies I mentioned earlier—is to maintain a spreadsheet of interesting firms that you come across over time. Assign one person on your team, preferably an analyst or someone with an analytical mind, to be in charge of the spreadsheet and research each firm as it is added. Then, as you and others in the organization run across interesting companies at conferences, in the trade press, in speeches, when talking to others in the industry, or anywhere else, forward their names to the keeper of the spreadsheet to be researched and entered. I'll often have the list-keeper send me a blurb on the company so that I can get a better idea of what it does for a living. If the company looks interesting, I might ask them to give us a short presentation so we understand their capabilities better. Information from this presentation would be entered into the spreadsheet along with any details gleaned from internet and industry sources. By keeping the spreadsheet up to date, we always have a universe of companies to choose from when the time is right for an acquisition.

I can hear you asking, "How do you know when the time is right?"

In my experience, there is never a bad time to add a good company with excellent capabilities to your stable. We're always in the market to buy something. That doesn't mean that we buy everything that comes down the road or are closing new acquisitions every month. Sometimes we have things going on internally that are taking our attention. If we've recently made a large acquisition, we'll step back to give ourselves time to integrate the new teams before looking to add another company. You have to make sure you are getting good value for your money, so every now and then we'll take a break and assess how the company is doing. But we always have our eye out for the next acquisition. We wouldn't want to miss the perfect piece to complete our business plan puzzle if it suddenly becomes available.

An effective growth strategy recognizes that M&A transactions and organic growth can both drive expansion. Determining which road to take in any particular situation is critical for an optimal return on investment. There are many questions that need to be answered before proceeding with an M&A—and we'll go through those questions throughout the book—but in general, an M&A strategy makes sense if all or most of the target's products and services can fill gaps in the acquirer's capabilities and if the acquirer's strengths can benefit target company's growth projections. If you can say that is the case, then it's time to dive deeper and see if the values and cultures match.

> **We always have our eye out for the next acquisition. We wouldn't want to miss the perfect piece to complete our business plan puzzle if it suddenly becomes available.**

KEY TAKEAWAY

M&As provide a set of benefits that can accelerate a company's growth and revenue stream—but they are not easy to execute. Knowing why so many M&As fail, which we'll examine in the next chapter, is the key to achieving those promised benefits and being part of the 20 percent that do succeed.

CASE STUDY

iCrossing acquires Spannerworks

Deal Size: >$10 million

Purpose: To give iCrossing a European footprint

Outcome: Spannerworks was successfully integrated and the new entity grew into one of the largest digital advertising agencies in the world.

In 2007 iCrossing was one of the leading US-based players in digital marketing. That was quite an achievement, but as COO at the time, I knew that if iCrossing wanted to be a global player, it needed to expand into overseas markets. There were only two ways to do that: open their own offices in attractive markets or buy companies that were already operating where iCrossing wanted to be. Growing organically in foreign markets is extremely difficult. Companies face cultural, regulatory, and language hurdles, in addition to the standard challenges of growing a business. Each new office is more similar to a start-up than an established business, meaning it could take years before you begin to see progress. Given all that, the decision to buy a native company already operating in the European market made the most sense.

We knew the type of company we were looking for, and Spannerworks, a search-based digital marketing agency headquartered in Brighton, UK, fit the bill. Both companies were about ten years old. Both had substantial market shares and relatively strong balance sheets. In addition, our capabilities were a good match. A lot of merger teams would stop at this point and move ahead with the deal. But I've seen way too many mergers flounder because the personalities of the founders clashed or the cultures were at odds. To prevent that type of mismatch, I arranged for the founders to meet in Paris for a meet and greet. They were able to discuss their corporate values and culture, as well as where they saw their firms in five or ten years. Over a good meal, they talked candidly about their challenges and what they were doing to resolve them. By the end of the week, the founders had bonded over a shared vision of what the two companies could do as one. They had discovered that not only did they like each other, they also believed they could trust each other. When the acquisition proceeded, it was with the knowledge that management was firmly on board and that the founder of Spannerworks would stay to run the UK operations.

Within a year Spannerworks had been rebranded as iCrossing UK and fully integrated into the iCrossing brand. I don't think this integration would have gone as smoothly as it did if the founders hadn't met and gotten to know each other well before the acquisition was finalized.

CASE STUDY

SiriusXM acquires Stitcher

Deal Size: $325 million

Purpose: To add a product line and enter a new market

Outcome: To be determined

In 2020 satellite streaming music provider SiriusXM acquired the podcast pioneer Stitcher from E. W. Scripps. The Stitcher app provides podcast content, as well as the ability to sell advertising and distribute content to other platforms. It's not easy to build podcasting into a profitable business. But this deal meant thousands of already popular podcasts would move to the SiriusXM stable, including titles like *Freakonomics Radio, How Did This Get Made?, Office Ladies, Conan O'Brien Needs a Friend, Literally! with Rob Lowe, LeVar Burton Reads, Comedy Bang! Bang!,* and *WTF with Marc Maron.*

Stitcher was an attractive acquisition target because it filled a gap in SiriusXM's offerings. The satellite content provider could now offer its listeners original podcasts to complement its music, sports, and talk programs. Deloitte has estimated that podcasting will break $1.1 billion in revenues in 2020. Podcasting is a fast-growth sector in the entertainment industry. In addition to SiriusXM, other music streaming businesses, such as Spotify and iHeartMedia, are scooping up podcasting content to complement those offerings to expand both their audiences and their audience engagement.

SUCCESS OR FAILURE?

As of early 2021, the jury is still out on whether this acquisition will play out as expected. SiriusXM hopes to use its sales force to drive additional ad sales on Stitcher's network. Stitcher hopes to use SiriusXM's much larger fan base to expand its reach. The match looks good on paper. If the cultures also mesh, this should be one of the successful acquisitions.

CHAPTER TWO

WHY DO MOST MERGERS AND ACQUISITIONS FAIL?

When I was CEO and COO of iCrossing, our growth strategy was based on acquisitions. There were a lot of very good companies out there that had technologies, processes, and customer bases that would be almost immediately accretive to iCrossing. Acquiring a few of these companies to expand iCrossing's products or geographic reach was more time-effective than trying to grow or duplicate those strengths in-house. One of the firms that caught my eye was Sharp Analytics.

The company was relatively small, but its competencies looked like they would fill a couple of gaps in iCrossing's offerings with regard to reporting. We expected it would be an easy, straightforward acquisition, but I made a very common mistake. Because the deal was smaller than others we were involved in, I didn't give it as much attention as I usually do. I liked the people at Sharp and didn't verify some of their purported reporting capabilities as well as I should have. It turned out the technology wasn't quite as robust as I had been led to believe. The truth about the technology had been stretched further than it should have in order to close a deal. Things eventually worked out, but the transition was much bumpier than it needed to be. In addition, because the technology was not what I thought it would be, it did not complement iCrossing's capabilities the way we expected. Although this acquisition was not an outright failure—iCrossing was still able to access some technologies it did not already have—it certainly wasn't the success we had projected.

And that is an important point to note when talking about M&A successes and failures. We tend to look at M&A transactions in terms of success. If they don't reach every projected goal, then we often think of them as failures. This assessment is too harsh in many cases.

Some acquisitions are obvious successes. Others are unmistakable failures. Sometimes a deal starts out looking good but then cracks begin to appear as time goes on. The EDS / AT Kearney deal (Case study on page 39) is an example of an acquisition that started strong and looked good for a short while but eventually couldn't overcome a changing economic climate and clashing cultures.

More often, however, acquisitions aren't total successes or failures—they lie some place in the middle, just as the Sharp acquisition did. Many of these fair-to-middling deals likely could have moved closer to the success end of the spectrum with just a few tweaks.

If there was only one reason M&A transactions fail, we'd all just solve that problem and be done with it. But the truth is, there are multiple reasons an acquisition might not live up to expectations. In fact, when doing a postmortem on a deal that goes south, you will normally find several problem areas.

HOW IT TYPICALLY WORKS

Most companies are not in the M&A business. If they are a professional services business, they focus on customer service. If they are in a manufacturing business, they focus on making things. M&As require an entirely different skill set, one not many people have simply because most leadership teams are rarely involved in a merger or acquisition.

So, when they begin the acquisition process, they tend to fall back on skills they have, which might not be the right ones for the situation. For example, a professional services company might want to expand into a new geographic area. However, they don't have the background or contacts to know which available companies would complement their own, so they reach out to the shiniest or highest-profile company in the region. Their entire focus is usually on growth goals, and they, therefore, do the minimum of due diligence because they have already chosen their target. Culture and values rarely, if ever, come into the equation because the acquiring team simply doesn't have the skills to analyze those factors. They are focused on bottom-line, financial aspects. If those look good, they close the deal.

Then what happens? The organizations never unify because financials aren't a source of unification. You don't unify data sets. You unify people. That often means that after the deal closes, key staff and leadership begin to leave. It is often the best people who leave first because they can easily find other positions. They not only take their skills with them but institutional knowledge and customers as well. With the exodus of key personnel, the culture begins to deteriorate. The new entity becomes a company of multiple cultures, which overall has a toxic effect. Reacting to these issues, leadership throws money at the problem with various initiatives that achieve little. Typically, it doesn't solve the problem because leadership has not defined the actual problem. Instead, most companies try to pursue growth without taking values and culture into account. A year later the transaction has fallen short of all expectations.

It doesn't have to be this way.

SOME COMMON MISMATCHES

It would be so much easier to prevent failures if there were just one or two primary causes. Unfortunately, a lot of things can go wrong. It's not common for financial records or market growth potential to be grossly misinterpreted, so I'm not going to go into the standard due diligence checklist in detail. Nor am I going to spend time on things that are out of our control, such as COVID-19 financial crashes, that cause deals to go sideways. There's not much you can do about those. I'm also not going to spend time on the oddball events that we read about on rare occasions, such as finding out at closing that the CFO has embezzled a million dollars and run off to the Caymans. Instead, this book is going to focus on those things that go wrong way too often, but shouldn't. And when you boil these negative drivers down to their essence, you'll often find out that they share a number of similarities, all revolving around how the company deals with people—its employees, its customers, its community, and so on. It's easy to fill out financial surveys. Numbers are numbers. But people are quirky. How a company handles its people connections—and how its methods line up with your methods—can make a huge difference in how successful an M&A transaction turns out to be.

To get to the heart of how a company handles its people, you need to ask questions. Lots and lots of questions. In fact, one of the things that has probably sunk more deals than any other is not asking the right questions. Or, in the same vein, some people ask the question but don't really listen to the answer. For example, during discovery, both firms can easily say they want to focus on growing market share, but one might have a culture of growing at the expense of everything, including profits, while the other is more conservative with their resources. If you do not ask the question "What does your growth strategy look like?" and then follow up with questions that pull out all the details, it is likely you'll end up with two companies at war with each other as they each try to execute their visions.

Another common misstep is misreading the market. We talk about market share all the time, but we are really talking about people and behavior. If we are changing people's perceptions of a company via an acquisition, we have to make sure we have a good idea how consumers are going to react. For example, two standout firms might not realize that merging with a competitor would dilute each firm's brand and differentiation advantages. Instead of one strong brand, you now have a marriage of opposing brands and a confused target market. The Daimler-Chrysler merger is a prime example of this. The merger tried to marry a European high-end car manufacturer with an American middle-market manufacturer. The rationale for the merger of two unrelated brands usually revolves around the belief that serving the broadest universe possible will make the company stronger. The marketplace, however, rarely sees it that way. Most buyers don't want to look through a variety of unnecessary choices to find the one thing they want. If they want a screwdriver, they don't want to have to search through an entire toolbox. If they want a middle-market car, they don't want to deal with a luxury car dealer. This particular merger did nothing but confuse consumers because they no longer knew what the company stood for.

One of the prime reasons things go wrong, and ironically one of the things that is least often investigated, is corporate values. A focus on values is particularly important when talking about professional services companies. In this case, we aren't counting the number of widgets rolling off an assembly line. We are dealing with relationships, corporate cultures, and making employees feel part of the new entity.

If you talk to people doing M&As, they will almost always mention the importance of values and culture. Do a quick Google search for why M&As fail, and you will find pages of articles noting the importance of complementary and synergistic values. Yet, according to a survey by Equiteq, the top six business attributes assessed by buyers during due diligence are:

- Quantitative attributes—revenue growth, EBITDA margin, EBITDA growth

- Qualitative attributes—size and quality of client base, quality of management, strategy of the business

These six business attributes have held steady for the past several years. Please notice that nowhere in those six attributes is "values" or "culture."

It's not that people don't know that values are important. It's more that they don't know how to measure or fit them into a due diligence checklist. Because they are not easy to quantify, companies tend to overlook them, often to the deal's detriment.

VALUES DRIVE A COMPANY

Values and culture cover a lot more than you think. They are not squishy, pie-in-the-sky concepts. They are measurable and observable—if you know what you are looking for.

At this point I should probably back up and explain what I mean when I talk about values. From my first book with Fran Biderman-Gross: "Values are culture in action. Values underpin the entire organization."

> **A company's values are how it runs its business.**

By my definition, a company's values are how it runs its business. Values are based on data and psychology. They are the immovable object in your life and your business.

Values are:

- Actionable statements that direct behavior

- The essence of how everyone in your organization does things

- Simple decision-making filters

Values are not:

- Descriptions of the work you do

- Strategies you employ to accomplish the mission

- Competencies, technical or otherwise

Or two companies might value "respect," but when you look at how they are led, this value is executed in diametrically opposing ways. Respect at one company might manifest itself through a strict hierarchy of top-down management, corporate titles, and silo-like divisions of power. If a superior makes a decision, it is carried out. Respect at another company might mean treating everyone as an adult who is able to manage their own time and doesn't need to get permission to take a day off or come in a bit late. Managerial lines might be flat, and it is expected that decisions will be questioned. So, same value, different execution. And that difference could have a profound effect when trying to integrate the two companies.

Communication is a value that is crucial in M&A transactions, as well as for a well-run company. For an acquisition transaction to work, everyone from the CEO to the newest hire needs to buy in and be willing to make whatever changes are necessary to integrate the two companies. To achieve this, employees need to be brought into the conversation at some point—and this doesn't always happen, despite everyone claiming their corporate culture is based on honest communication and transparency.

I once experienced an extreme example of a company that professed to value transparency but did just the opposite. We had just closed our first acquisition at iCrossing, a company called NewGate Internet. As it was our first, it was really important that we got this one right to set the stage for the growth strategy we had planned. The founder of iCrossing, Jeff Herzog, and I thought we had done a fantastic job dotting our i's and crossing our t's. As soon as the deal closed, we traveled to NewGate's headquarters in Sausalito, CA, to introduce ourselves to the staff. The founder of NewGate had called a company-wide meeting. He met us at the front door and assured us that everyone was excited to meet us and hear our plans for the combined company. We were just as excited to get up in front of employees and present a united front with the current owner.

So, as we were standing over to the side, the owner got up in front of the sixty-five or so people in the room and started his introduction.

"Good morning, everyone. None of you are aware of this, but I've been trying to sell the company for the last six months, and I've been fortunate enough to find a buyer. That buyer is with us today.

This is Jeff and this is Don, and this is my last day. I'm retiring. So I wish you all the best, and thank you for your past ten years of service."

And he literally left the meeting, walked out the side door, and never came back.

That left Jeff and me standing in front of sixty-five people whom we didn't know from anybody, wondering what we were going to do now. This was a disaster in the making. We had assumed that the founder had informed his people of the sale, explained how they would benefit, and would remain in place long enough for a smooth integration. Instead, we now owned a company full of people who had no reason to trust us and were wondering if they all still had a job.

We had told everybody on our end, "We're buying this company. It's going to be a good thing." So, all of our staff knew that we had this acquisition going on, and he hadn't told a soul on his end.

As luck would have it, there was a person in the back of the room who had come from iCrossing the previous month to work with NewGate. He spoke up and saved the day.

"Hey, Don, good to see you, man. It's such a small world. You're a great guy, and I can't wait to work with you again." That broke the ice. With that endorsement, the other employees were willing to give us a chance. Jeff and I spent the rest of the day talking to everyone and getting to know them, explaining our vision for the merged companies and asking for their insights. The integration took longer than it should have because of the cold open, but it eventually all worked out. However, I'll never forget the look on Jeff's face, nor will he forget the look on mine, when that guy headed for the exit.

This was an extreme case, but it's not unusual for executive teams to hold their cards too close to the vest. It's a fine line to walk between divulging sensitive confidential information too soon and keeping your employees in the dark for too long. You need to keep a lid on things through most of the process, but at some point, you have to balance off this need for confidentiality and sensitivity with the need to communicate with the proper individuals. Before you close the deal, you have to start opening it up to other individuals who are going to be affected in the organization. Otherwise, this group of individuals critical for integration success could well feel disenfranchised and not be as committed as you need going forward.

Sometimes—actually, way too many times—companies claim they are built on specific values, but far too often, I find it to be just lip service. When you walk into any corporate break room or copy room, you will see a nicely printed, laminated sign with the corporate values. Ask the employees in the room having their lunch how those values show up or present themselves in their everyday work life and most will mumble something about making the company a better place. What they typically won't come up with is specific examples of how "passion" or "being number one" are part of their workday.

Corporate values run through the company from top to bottom. They are something we all share. They might not be the ones listed on the wall, but they are there. And to increase your chances of being part of a successful acquisition, you need to not only dive into the target company's values but also, first, know what yours are. Don't look at the list on the wall. Stand back and observe interactions. What the company truly values will become obvious, if you know what to look for.

LOOK FOR FIT

Values involve people. Thus understanding the (shared) values of a target company involves talking to its executive team. Companies take their lead from their leaders, so I always sit down with my counterpart at the company we are looking to acquire, or that is acquiring us. This is a step that is often skipped and could avert a lot of slow starts or outright failures if it were a standard part of due diligence. I try to make the meeting informal—over drinks or dinner—but the questions I'm looking to have answered are possibly the most important in the entire process.

First of all, do the exec teams get along? Do I click with the other company's CEO? Do I see myself enjoying working with them? Do I see myself enjoying the occasional lunch? If the other CEO and I can't find common ground, it is unlikely that the companies themselves are a good match. As I said before, companies take their cues and their values from the top. If the tops clash, the companies will too.

Once we have developed a rapport, I dig deeper. Do our visions align? Can the two of us articulate our visions of what the company could look like five years out if we were to work together?

Do our leadership styles mesh? What's important to each of us as CEOs? How do we each lead our people? The goal is to get a sense of how they value people and how they like to lead. I'm a very participative person. I don't tell people what to do, but I make a lot of suggestions. If the other CEO has a more controlling style, we might end up with a lot of unhappy employees.

Another area I like to look into is the history of the company. I'll ask, "When you founded the company, what were you trying to accomplish? How well have you done?" These are not short conversations. You want to spend enough time to really understand the history of who you're buying and why the founder or CEO did some of the things that they did. It's not uncommon for the other CEO to come back the next day and say, "I really hadn't thought about some of the things we were talking about, but you got me thinking. I don't think some of my answers went deep enough or were entirely spot on. Do you have time to sit down again today and talk some more?" At this point, we are getting down to the nitty gritty. My advice: don't rush the process. What happens at this stage is critical to the successful outcome of this transaction. Keep your eye on the goal. Take all the time you need to understand the company you are buying.

At the same time, you have to assume the other company is assessing your values and how you run your business. Are you in a position to articulate those values? Can you provide your counterpart with a detailed vision of your plans for the future? These are the things we'll dive into in the next chapter. After all, it doesn't do a lot of good to know all about the target company's values if you don't know your own.

Why don't more businesses factor values more strongly into their overall M&A approach? Why don't they assess another company's values more carefully as part of due diligence? Based on my experience, companies trip over two stumbling blocks:

1. Many CEOs don't take corporate values seriously.

A CEO's day is full. There is rarely a time when they aren't meeting with or on the phone with someone. There are fires to put out and decisions to be made. Only the most important things are brought to the CEO's attention because there isn't time for anything else. That means if a CEO is going to focus on values during an acquisition deal, they have to consider them important. Typically, any deal starts and ends with two CEOs talking with each other. All too often this turns out to be a meet-and-greet after the decision has been made to proceed. If the CEOs both were serious about values compatibility, they would need to sit down personally and have a frank conversation early on to assess each other's corporate values. Can both CEOs discuss their values fluently? Can they share evidence of how they share those values with their people and ensure that people's actions reflect those values? Let me assure you that you can tell right away whether your two companies are aligned when you have that conversation at the CEO level. But the problem is that CEOs don't have that conversation because they don't consider values as important as financials, which creates a gaping blind spot from the start.

2. The people who understand values and culture lack a voice.

Usually, CEOs put the finance team in the driver's seat when they size up a potential merger. They assign someone like their chief strategy officer to study how well their capabilities and strategies align. But unfortunately the people who are supposed to be the voice of a company's culture and values—usually HR—are brought in late in the decision-making process and relegated to the role of sizing up staff numbers to identify areas of overlap. This mindset needs to change. CEOs need to identify a values advocate with the specific job of assessing culture fit. And the advocate must have a seat at the table.

Having a values advocate isn't a role most CEOs are familiar with. They are already dealing with financial officers, marketing officers, business development specialists, attorneys, accountants, and others. Do they really need to add another layer of complexity? Yes, yes they do. A failure to align values has serious consequences, such as:

1. Loss of key talent who reject the acquisition

2. Internal discord as the two entities realize their people do not work well together because their values are incompatible

3. Client relationships damaged by internal discord

4. A blow to your reputation as employees share their strife on sites such as Glassdoor

5. A failure to execute on strategy while your business gets mired in cultural problems

6. A failure to create better services and products because your people cannot work together

Who wants those problems?

To avoid falling into this trap, I recommend a mindset change. First, take a step back and understand that an acquisition is difficult to pull off even under the best of circumstances. Don't allow yourself to get seduced by the myth that M&A deals are inherently good to do. They may or may not be. There are real risks involved, and incompatible values is one of them.

As noted above, both CEOs involved need to include values in their due diligence checklist.

Secondly, assign an M&A values gatekeeper the job of creating a process for assessing values compatibility in the entire M&A arc— from assessing a company to managing the transition to setting yourself up for long-term success down the road.

Finally, get agreement at the very beginning from all of the key decision makers that you will be willing to cancel the deal if your team sees incompatible values. Incompatible values are the definition of a deal breaker. Treat them that way.

Values aren't the only measure of a successful transaction. But you need to make values an essential component to have a fighting chance.

KEY TAKEAWAY

- Avoid at all costs the values-void M&A deal.

- If you spend the time to get the "people" part of the equation right and less time doing the financial engineering that most acquisitions involve, especially in professional services, you stand a much higher chance of long-term success. I don't buy anybody that I just can't relate to. And that is the real secret to M&A success.

CASE STUDY

Electronic Data Systems (EDS) acquires AT Kearney

Deal Size: $596 million

Goal: Become a one-stop shop for both consultancy and information technology services

Outcome: AT Kearney completed a management buyback ten years later

In 1995 Electronic Data Systems (EDS), a US information technology services group, bought AT Kearney, a global strategy consultancy. This was the first (but not the last) time a tech services group had attempted to bring a consultancy group in house. The goal for EDS was to create a one-stop shop where it could sell consultancy services and then access those consulting clients to sell its core outsourcing and integration skills. In addition, AT Kearney's consulting business was fast growth and high margin, which was predicted to improve EDS's bottom line. EDS envisioned being able to use AT Kearney to compete with the McKinseys and Booz Allens of the world.

From the AT Kearney side, the acquisition would bring in EDS's financial backing to help fund expansion and IT competencies that the consulting firm had been looking for. In addition, it gave several of the long-term partners a chance to cash out and go on to other ventures.

Accountants, finance teams, and lawyers spent hundreds of hours making sure all the paperwork was in order. This was a marriage between unlikely partners, and everyone was invested in making sure the integration went smoothly. With that much attention to detail, what could go wrong? Turned out a lot.

Although both companies were enthusiastic about the deal, there were some concerns from the beginning that culture and value differences would be hard to overcome. EDS had been founded by Ross Perot and took its values from him. It was almost a military organization. You did what you were told. Success wasn't necessarily based upon stellar individual performances. It was based upon how you produced as a team. EDS was run with a bureaucratic, top-down style.

On the other hand, AT Kearney emphasized an entrepreneurial style. It was run more as an individual-based organization by very smart partners. There was a CEO, but he was elected by the partners. It wasn't one big company; It was more like fifty small companies because all the partners had their own teams and were off doing their own thing. Those who succeeded were the ones who billed the most.

WHAT HAPPENED

EDS tried to make AT Kearney part of their organization by imposing their top-down management model. The consulting firm's compensation plan was adjusted to be more in line with EDS's, and much of its back-office functions were consolidated with the tech services firm's. Within the first three years, the new entity shed thirteen thousand jobs. These changes not only led to more than a few disgruntled AT Kearney employees but also grated on the AT Kearney CEO, Frederick Steingraber, who had been led to believe this was a merger of equals. The partners pushed back on EDS's attempts to bring them into the fold and continued to do things their way.

However, even though the transition was bumpy, it looked like the end result would put this acquisition in the win column. For the first five years, AT Kearney rode the growing management consulting market to record revenues. Then came the tech bubble crash of 2000. Both companies went into free fall. The drop in the market brought the dysfunction of their cultures into stark relief. The firms had never really bonded as one strong company, and their combined weaknesses were dragging them down.

Over the next couple of years, EDS tried to stop the bleeding by replacing management, laying off another 20 percent of AT Kearney's employees, restructuring the company, and moving the consultant's headquarters from Texas to Chicago. But the companies continued to struggle. By 2005 AT Kearney was not just experiencing falling revenues but also operating at a loss.

At this point a group of AT Kearney executives put together a management buyout and took the consultancy back to its roots. Seven months later AT Kearney reported a 15 percent increase in revenues and a 25 percent increase in profits.

SUCCESS OR FAILURE?

Corporate culture and the personal qualities of individual leaders play a critical role in every merger. The EDS / AT Kearney combination always struggled to find its footing. Clashes in personalities, culture, and values were overshadowed in the beginning, when a strong economy drove returns. But the fragile nature of the combined entity was exposed when the market turned. Many if not most M&A transactions are at least partially successful. This one was, too, at least for the first few years. But if your definition of a successful merger is one that is thriving and growing in the long term, the EDS / AT Kearney deal would find itself firmly relegated to the fail column.

CASE STUDY

Hewlett-Packard (HP) acquires Electronic Data Services (EDS)

Deal Size: $13.9 billion

Purpose: To increase HP market share

Outcome: Four years after acquisition, HP wrote off an $8 billion loss in EDS value

---

In 2008 Hewlett-Packard wanted badly to compete with IBM, the market leader in computer and IT services. In an attempt to catapult itself past the competition, HP acquired EDS for $13.9 billion. At the time EDS was one of the premier IT services companies in the world, with a list of top-tier customers. Unfortunately, the acquisition not only did not increase HP market share, it actually decreased revenues. Four years later HP ended up devaluing EDS and taking an $8 billion write-off.

Certainly, the great financial crisis played a large part in the loss of value. And the computer world was changing. Desktops were replacing mainframes, and much of what EDS had always done for customers could now be done in-house. But EDS might have survived these hurdles if it hadn't been weakened by the merger.

Although HP had its eye on EDS's revenues and customers, it really didn't understand the EDS way of doing business. EDS had a culture built on talented professionals and strong, long-term customer relationships. That culture was disrupted when HP made thousands of job cuts to raise cash. As the company moved from a long-term customer-service focus to a short-term revenue focus, additional professionals left. When you lose talent in a services business, you have a different company.

In addition, the management structures differed. EDS had a bureaucratic, top-down structure. It had taken on the autocratic personality of its founder, Ross Perot. On the other hand, Hewlett-Packard empowered employees to make their own decisions, which resulted in an environment of innovation. These differences in the organizational structure hindered the integration of the activities of both companies.

Business strategies also differed. While HP was focused on IT software and hardware, EDS was focused on business processing out-sourcing (BPO), which required building long-term and deep customer relationships. HP did not understand that BPO needed constant invest-ment. Instead, it used its revenues to fund the investment portfolio focused on acquiring additional companies.

SUCCESS OR FAILURE?

The two companies were never able to overcome their cultural and strategic differences. In 2008 HP announced that it was taking an $8 billion write-off on the deal. Today the EDS name has disappeared as its functions were integrated into other HP computer divisions.

PREPARE BOTH COMPANIES TO CLOSE THE DEAL

PART I

In the previous chapters, we talked about why professional services firms continue to be involved in M&A transactions despite their abysmal success rate. It's because when the acquisitions are good, they are very, very good, and hope springs eternal in the corporate boardroom. We also looked at why so many acquisitions turn out to be very, very bad—a lack of emphasis on complementary values. So, we understand the problem. Now it's time for the solution. The next two chapters will guide you through how to define your own corporate values and then how to determine if they mesh with those of the company you want to acquire or that wants to acquire you. These two chapters are the foundation for everything that follows. If you get this part right, chances are very good you'll get the acquisition right as well.

CHAPTER THREE

KNOW YOURSELF

When I first started working, values were something that you gave lip service to but didn't really think about. The only place that values played in your day-to-day environment was at meetings in a corporate conference room. No, you didn't discuss values at the meetings. You sat in front of a values plaque. You might read it, you might not, but every company had a plaque on the wall that listed their values. And that was pretty much the commitment any company made to implementing values-based decisions.

Most executives don't fully understand the values and culture of their company. And that is understandable. It's their job to prioritize growth, and values don't easily fit into their vision of growth. For most companies, growth is measured via increased billable hours and improved margins.

Today's workers have changed that approach. The millennial generation, particularly, has had a tremendous impact on work culture. While I came out of school happy to have a job, they came out of school asking, "Why?" Why are you in business? Why do you do what you do? What are your profits being used for? What do you stand for?" It all boils down to: What do you believe in, and what are your values as a corporation?

Many in this cohort want to work for a company that stands for something that they can get behind. They want to work for a company that stands for something that they can believe in. They want to be valued for their contribution, and that fulfills them. And so they ask questions. If you're not prepared to answer them, then you will lose some of these very talented people to an organization that can clearly articulate them.

So, what does this have to do with acquisitions? Knowing what you believe in and stand for has everything to do with successful acquisitions. As mentioned in the preceding chapters, many M&A transactions fail because values clash. Thus, when approaching an M&A checklist, you need to make sure you are analyzing the other company's values as well as its bottom line and growth strategies.

To understand another company's values, you first have to understand your own. If you don't know your purpose and values, it's time to figure them out. If they are just lifeless words on a conference room wall, it is time to breathe some life into them. As noted earlier, ignoring values—yours and the other company's—is the prime driver in acquisitions failing to live up to their billing.

WHAT IS A CORPORATE VALUE?

If you've never really thought about values, it might be helpful to define what we are talking about. Values are not navel-gazing qualities that sound nice but have no tangible corporate benefit. They are, instead, the qualities that make your company unique. They are the drivers of your success. As such, you want to dig down until you hit on those that resonate with you and your employees. When you step back and look at how your company works, what do you see? How do you put

> **Values are the qualities that make your company unique. They are the drivers of your success.**

what you see in words? And how do you know what you see is a result of values and not just standard processes?

When articulating your corporate values, keep in mind what values are and are not.

Values are:

- Actionable statements that direct behavior

- The essence of how everyone in your organization does things

- Simple decision-making filters or tools

Values are not:

- Descriptions of the work you do

- Strategies you employ to accomplish the mission

- Competencies, technical or otherwise

In addition to understanding the definition of corporate values as outlined above, it also helps to know that there are two types of values—core and shared.

- Core values are individual values developed from your own personal strengths. True core values start with the strengths of the corporate visionary—possibly you! While there are many exercises on the internet that claim to assist you in defining your values, there really is no good shortcut here. You don't want to choose from what other people consider to be values; you want to uncover your existing, authentic values.

- Shared values are created by transforming your core values into business-oriented values or blending the core values of the top-level leadership. Shared values are actionable and most stem from the organic nature of the company itself.

DEFINING YOUR COMPANY'S VALUES

Articulating your company's values is not a straightforward, easy process. You are not simply manipulating variables in a software program and generating a list of your corporate values at the end. Instead, determining the values that drive your company is an iterative process involving multiple stakeholders. Although there are undoubtedly several paths that a company can take to determine its important values, the way we approached the task at Investis Digital is a good example of the amount of work involved.

When we were looking at defining Investis Digital's values, we set aside a day for the executive team to meet without outside distractions. As CEO, I explained what we were doing and what we hoped to accomplish at the end. I'm sure at least a couple of people on the team wondered why we were focused on this when we had a business to run, but as the leader, it was up to me to get them on board and convince them that this was a very important part of running the business.

We started by asking questions that would help us define the company.

- What is important to us?

- What makes us proud to be part of Investis?

- How do we want our clients to view us?

- What do we stand for?

- Why do people come to us?

- Why do people want to work with us?

- What are we considered best at?

- Why do people trust us?

Once we had a list of questions that seemed to get to the essence of what we did, we began listing actionable, measurable short-phrase answers. Nothing was off the table at this time, but the values had to be tangible. We didn't want just one-word answers—kindness, respect, flexibility, and the like. We wanted them to connote movement and growth, which all companies need to succeed.

When we had run out of new ideas, we organized the suggestions into categories. Just going through the list and deciding how they should be grouped helped us visualize which ones were important and which ones weren't.

We got our list down to seven or eight phrases that seemed to encapsulate the values that we wanted to promote at Investis Digital. It's important to note that these seven or eight values were not aspirational. We weren't trying to define a Camelot-like culture. We were defining the actual values that we saw driving Investis Digital.

After we had cut the list to the handful of values that we all thought applied to Investis Digital, we had everyone prioritize them.

Now came the hardest part. We went around the table and back and forth until we agreed on the five most important and impactful values.

- Embrace Clarity

- Bring Passion

- Inspire Greatness

- Keep Innovating

- Measure Success

When we walked out of that room, we were exhausted. We had spent hours thinking, talking, having eureka moments, and psycho-analyzing the company that many of the execs had been with for a number of years. When you are delving into the core of a company, you can sometimes find things you didn't expect. For example, is the casualness and easygoing camaraderie you see among team members driven by respect or by a lack of respect? Is a culture of afterwork happy hours that can go well into the night a sign of commitment to the team or a lack of commitment to work? Are heated discussions a sign of passion, or do they prevent others from putting forth good ideas? It is not unusual to hear members of your exec team posit different viewpoints and form different judgments on what they see in their day-to-day dealings with employees and customers. The job of the CEO will be to lead the team to a consensus.

Once we had our five values, we needed to see if we had gotten them right. You can sometimes end up in an echo chamber if everything is done in the board room, and we wanted to make sure that the company we were seeing was the company others saw as well. So, we sent our list out to a number of staff and longtime clients. We asked them all: "What do you think? Are these values you associate with Investis?" The feedback was universally positive: "Yup. You've nailed it."

With that endorsement, we were ready to make sure the values permeated everything we did. And we could only do that if every employee, from the receptionist to the top engineer, bought into the premise that Investis Digital was unique and successful because it was built on these particular values. To buy into that premise, everyone had to know what the values were and really embrace them.

BRING VALUES TO LIFE

Once the executive team had settled on the values that said "Investis Digital," it was incumbent on us—and particularly on me as CEO—to communicate them within the company and make them part of everyday life. We did all the normal things that a company does when it wants to get information out to its employees. We sent emails outlining the values. We talked about the values in weekly newsletters. We posted them on the wall in areas frequented by employees. But we wanted to do more. We wanted to bring the values to life so employees could get to know and understand them in a much deeper way than they would if the values were just presented as a fait accompli list.

We came up with two activities, one for our London team and one for our New York team. The London team was broken into groups, with each taking one of the values.

Each team was asked to design an abstract painting that illustrated their assigned value. The goal of abstract art is to evoke emotions through color, line, and impressions, as opposed to realistic presentations. It seemed the perfect medium to express the five values because we wanted our employees to be emotionally attached to each one. Those paintings are now hanging on the walls in the London office.

Investis Digital Value: Bring Passion

Investis Digital Value: Embrace Clarity

Investis Digital Value: Measure Success

Investis Digital Value: Keep Innovating

Investis Digital Value: Inspire Greatness

Investis Digital Values in Song

We did something similar in New York, where we divided the group into five teams and asked each one to come up with a song that best described the characteristics of their assigned value. We then took the song titles and made a Billboard-type chart to hang in that office.

In both cases, the idea was to have the teams really think about the values. Internalize them. And come up with something that would impart the value to others.

These exercises were not meant to simply fill a couple of hours on a slow day. They were integral activities that helped everyone embrace the values, make them part of their vocabulary, and accept them as their own. These were values that had already been driving the company, but putting them into words helped clarify how and why we were succeeding. Once your employees understand what makes the company tick, a values-based culture emerges, creating a predictable and trustworthy culture.

BUILD ON SUCCESS

We felt really good about the activities our London and New York teams had participated in. We all walked away believing that we had accomplished our mission to align each person that worked for Investis Digital in playing an integral part of our value system. But you can't stop with a one-day retreat. You need to reinforce and reiterate your corporate values every chance you get. It might be acknowledging that somebody does something really spectacular on a project. It might be a compliment from a client. It might be an explanation of why we are changing a process to more closely align it with one or more values. Sometimes I'll spend some time at a company meeting or presentation pointing out how a value plays out in real time. For example, "Bring Passion" can be seen in the employees who bring the same energy to their projects or assignments every day. It can be seen when you bring your best to customer service.

Or maybe I'll point out ways we've incorporated "Keep Innovating" in our activities this week. We're a tech company, so we are, by definition, always innovating our products. But I might also point out that a team has developed a new customer relations program that makes it easier to connect with clients and anticipate their needs. Or, in the days of COVID-19, I might have called out the hours our human relations team put into developing processes that allowed us to work while staying safe.

When we "Embrace Clarity," we make it easier for customers and others in the industry to understand how our technology helps them. We try to communicate in the clearest way possible. Too often people in our industry try to wow the clients and impress others with lots of buzzwords and complicated explanations. Einstein reportedly said, "If you can't say it simply, you don't understand it." We have taken that to heart and consciously implement it in every way we can, from presentations to memos to emails to project outlines.

Our "Measure Success" value is one of the most important. If you can't measure success, how do you know you are successful? Every project, every campaign, every client meeting needs to have metrics that tell us if we have been successful. It's not enough to "feel" like the meeting was a success. What metrics had you set out ahead of time that you needed to meet to declare it a success? Did the client need to ask for additional materials? Did the client need to ask for a demonstration? Was the client's willingness to talk again on a specific date enough to call it successful? Whatever the case, we always make sure we can have tangible metrics in place to tell us if we were successful or not.

The idea behind taking every opportunity to point out the Investis Digital values in action is to continuously demonstrate how values make the business better, so that we all have a reason to implement and benefit from them.

KEEP YOUR VALUES FRONT AND CENTER

When you make sure that everyone in your company knows what you stand for, you have set the foundation for a successful acquisition—but only if you also make sure you carry those values into the acquisition process.

> **When you make sure that everyone in your company knows what you stand for, you have set the foundation for a successful acquisition—but only if you also make sure you carry those values into the acquisition process.**

A lot of people compartmentalize their corporate activities into everyday activities and less common activities. The day-to-day responsibilities include things such as product development, sales, customer service, and all the other standard things that a company does to stay in business and grow. It is easy for the leadership team to see how values flow through these activities because it is the corporate values that drive the company.

The uncommon activities include things like M&A transactions. Because the processes and skill sets to participate in these deals are so different from those that routinely fill their day, execs often don't think about how they can apply their corporate values. And letting those values be pushed into the background, or overlooking them because the acquisition is so shiny and tempting, is the beginning of the end for the vast majority of transactions.

But we can change that trajectory. In the next chapter we'll introduce a values survey that should be part of every acquisition due diligence checklist. When paired with the values advocate that we suggested in the previous chapter, it will go a long way toward solving the problem of competing values.

KEY TAKEAWAY

- Values are not written; they are lived.

- Every company is driven by values, whether known or unknown.

- Before attempting to acquire another company, it is important to know your own values so you will know if they complement those of the company you are acquiring.

CASE STUDY

Hearst Corporation acquires iCrossing

Deal Size: $325 million

Purpose: To add digital marketing to the Hearst print capabilities

Outcome: To be determined

In 2010 print publishers, such as Hearst Corporation, Meredith, and Condé Nast, were realizing that they had to make the jump into digital or they would be left behind. To quickly get up to speed, Hearst acquired iCrossing, one of the largest independent digital marketing services providers in the world. The acquisition gave Hearst extensive global digital marketing capabilities, including paid search, search engine optimization, web development, mobile and social marketing, and data analytics. iCrossing, on the other hand, would continue to work with and grow its own client base, while simultaneously collaborating with other Hearst divisions to bring clients and consumers new and innovative digital content solutions.

So how did the acquisition work out? Not as well as expected.

iCrossing was a very attractive acquisition target, profitable and growing rapidly. As a result, it generated multiple bids when it put itself on the market. The bidding started a bit of a feeding frenzy among potential buyers, and ended with an up-front offer from the Hearst Corporation of $325 million. In addition, the deal allowed iCrossing to generate an earn-out of $125 million over the next three years, making the total deal worth $450 million. To prove the earn-out was reachable, Hearst officials provided iCrossing with a list of clients to whom they would provide introductions, as well as how much additional revenue they estimated iCrossing would receive from each client on the list. The publisher also told the digital marketer that it would incentivize its sales staff to help their iCrossing counterparts. iCrossing completed the transaction confident that the extra $125 million was nearly guaranteed.

Soon after the transaction closed, I was in a meeting with the CEO of Hearst and his execs. The CEO opened the meeting by saying, "I'd like to welcome Don and his team, but we paid too much for these guys. So, I want everyone on my team to make sure they don't get one dime of their earn-out because we've already paid more than enough."

So, in the first week, he stood right in front of me and took all the incentives that we were depending on off the table. That was the beginning of the end. You cannot have a successful acquisition without trust and respect.

As a result of the Hearst CEO's decision to backtrack on promised incentives, a smooth integration became nearly impossible. Nobody was working with us, and we weren't working with anybody. For example, the multibillion-dollar magazine ad sales team was supposed to facilitate introductions to their stable of clients. So, I went over to talk to the head of sales and work out a plan.

"Let me ask you, Don," the head of sales said, "why would I want to do this? If I introduce you to one of our clients, and that client spends one dollar on you, that's one dollar less that's going to go into magazine ads. If it doesn't go into magazine ads, I don't get paid. I don't get my bonuses. We don't get any value from helping you out."

Hearst did not really think about how they were going to integrate the two companies. They thought all they had to do was add a line to the org chart and all would work out. But they didn't see how some of the groups would clash. Hearst had a couple of ad hoc groups that did a few of the things that we did at iCrossing. We suggested that they move the ad hoc groups under iCrossing so we could work together, but they didn't want to do that. That meant that we were competing for the same clients—and the Hearst in-house groups had the support of the Hearst organization. We'd go into a prospect and find out these other groups had been in there a week before and had undercut our price. We were working with one hand tied behind our backs.

Integrating an acquired company takes planning. It takes incenting the teams to work together, to make introductions if needed, or to institute a pricing schedule that works for all the teams. That kind of conversation never took place.

Besides the lack of support, Hearst also tried to impose its corporate culture on iCrossing. Hearst had an autocratic, command-and-control culture, while iCrossing was much more entrepreneurial. Hearst placed iCrossing at the bottom of the hierarchy and imposed all kinds of oversight that just didn't work.

The two companies were never on the same track. Hearst was driven by selling magazines and advertising; iCrossing was driven by selling digital marketing services and thought Hearst had acquired them to be able to offer a new product line. In reality, Hearst wanted iCrossing to be a loss leader. They would say, "Don, we just sold a search project to a huge client. We had to basically give it away because they promised us another five million worth of ad sales if you could come in and do this for us." So, Hearst would make $5 million worth of ad sales, but iCrossing would make nothing. If you have spent years building a quality asset, the last thing you want to do is be a loss leader. You don't want to be giving your services away just so the parent company can sell more magazine ads. The entire deal was just not well conceived or received.

SUCCESS OR FAILURE?

The integration problems that occurred early on following the deal completion continue to this day, some ten years after the original deal was closed. As of the writing of this book, iCrossing is now quietly being folded into the Hearst Solutions and Services Group. Once a world leader in performance marketing, iCrossing has now lost its brand name in the market and is now nothing more than a small group focused on branded content for Hearst clients.

CHAPTER FOUR

ASSESS VALUES: THE SECRET TO DUE DILIGENCE

When I was at iCrossing in 2008, we were looking to merge with a digital creative agency by the name of AKQA, which was also owned by a private equity firm. If everything worked out, it would be the first time in the digital space that a world-class creative agency and world-class search agency came together under the same umbrella. It would be a game changer in the agency world. Everyone internally was excited about the synergies the two firms could realize, but there were some big questions as to how this would all work. Primarily, who was going to lead the charge? The AKQA investors wanted their guy to lead the combined firm, while the iCrossing investor group wanted me at the helm. It looked like we were in a managerial standoff. However, the two boards soon came up with a unique way of resolving this. They said, "Why don't we send you two off for a weekend? We want you guys to fly to Napa Valley, stay at a nice resort, drink wine all weekend, and get to know each other. Take time to understand each other and find out if you are compatible. Do you have similar sets of values? Do you even like each other? Could this work? Come back and report when you have an answer."

So, I went not knowing what to think about the whole thing. But after a few glasses of wine, we both opened up about what we believed was important in our respective companies, what our management styles were, how we liked to see a company work, what benefits we saw in a combined company, and what things we wanted to make sure weren't lost during an integration. We also spent a lot of time getting to know each other on a personal level. We talked about each of our families at length. We built a foundation of trust that allowed us to break through the leadership impasse. Our personal values were similar, which led me to believe our organizations could grow together as one.

When we got back, we had a plan. Because the AKQA CEO had been at AKQA for quite some time and wanted to do something else sooner rather than later, I was going to let him take the lead for a year, and then I was going to take over after that. We were quite satisfied with the plan, which would not have evolved had we not understood and trusted each other.

In the end the deal fell apart because both sides wanted too much of an ownership share, so it just broke down. But I am convinced that if the acquisition had been completed, it would have worked very well because the other CEO and I had taken the time to get to know each other and come to an agreement on the values and culture we wanted to promote in the combined entity.

When you do your due diligence in anticipation of an acquisition, it is relatively easy to assess the assets, financials, capabilities, and other measurable and observable features of your targeted firm. Integrating these functions is also straightforward. Back-office accounting is simply back-office accounting. Where many transactions break down is in analyzing and integrating the people. It is all about the people.

In the previous chapter, we talked about the importance of knowing the values that drive your own company before you attempt to acquire another. Now we'll look at how you can assess the values in a target firm and determine if they fit with yours. Even if the values aren't totally in line, researchers have found that simply doing a values survey increases the odds of successful mergers all by itself.[5] Finding a company that is a true fit obviously increases the odds even more.

WHAT IS FIT?

We've been talking about the importance of compatible values, but what does that mean? Obviously, it would be unlikely to find a company that has exactly the same values and culture that your company does. Those things grow organically, and unless the other company is an identical twin, there will be differences. In fact, you want some differences. Being challenged is how we grow, as people and as companies. When looking for an acquisition target, you want a company that brings something

---

5   Appelbaum, Steven H., Roberts, Jessie, and Shapiro, Barbara T. (2009) "Cultural Strategies in M&As: Investigating Ten Case Studies," *Journal of Executive Education*, Vol. 8: Issue 1, Article 3. Available at: http://digitalcommons.kennesaw.edu/jee/vol8/iss1/3.

different and new to the table. The trick is finding a company whose values are just different enough to enhance your company's but not so different that integration is impossible.

> **The trick is finding a company whose values are just different enough to enhance your company's but not so different that integration is impossible.**

There are several areas we can look at when looking for a good fit. In addition to culture, we also need to look at style, leadership, communication, and organization policies. A CEO's style, how leadership manifests itself, how policies and strategies are communicated—all are outward manifestations of a company's values. If the preferences for style of management, communication, growth strategies, and other management models point in the same direction, it is likely that the underlying values will also mesh.

When an acquisition team conducts a values survey during due diligence, it is usually looking to answer four broad questions:

- How open is the company to taking on new values and ideas?

- How open is the company to trusting a new partner or owner?

- How open is the company to working together for the greater good?

- How open is the company to sorting through issues, understanding differences, and wanting to work through differences?

Let's look at these areas in more detail.

To be flexible and open to new ideas and ways of doing things is tremendously important. It's not unusual for a large firm to acquire a smaller one and then try to change everything that made that small firm so attractive, and that's not good. But there will undoubtedly be some changes that need to be made if the goal is to integrate the new firm. It doesn't always have to be the acquired firm that changes. If the new firm has a better customer service process or better account tracking process, the acquiring firm might very well adopt that process. If you think you have all the answers and the other side has none—meaning, if you believe all your processes are world-class and the other side doesn't have anything to contribute—then you're going to be way off. You are looking to buy a specific company because they do something well, which means they've organized their workflows and their work processes in an effective manner. Before you start to make wholesale changes, you really need to understand what they do well and consider whether you need to redo your own processes, because maybe they do it better than you do. The best outcome is two firms that are both open to change and willing to adopt the best ideas and processes, no matter which firm they originated with.

Both companies need to enter the transaction from a place of trust. If either party is skeptical about the other's intentions, if employees aren't encouraged to take pride in their past history while being enthusiastic for the future, if one side thinks they are being taken advantage of—the acquisition will be doomed. It is critical for both sides to trust that the other is entering the transaction with the best of intentions and to work to support a viable partnership.

When I acquire a company, I want the leadership of that entity to work as hard to make the transaction work as I will. Not only do you want to see what they bring to you, but you also want to understand how you can help them. Transactions based on mutual dependence or benefits are much more likely to see everyone putting in the hard work of overcoming hurdles than those where one company was only looking for a payout for management.

I don't think I've ever been part of an M&A deal that didn't require some adjustment after the closing. I doubt anyone else has either. What kept these deals from being failures was the willingness of both sides to recognize there was an issue and work to resolve it. In other words, the company being acquired needs to be willing to be integrated, while the acquiring company needed to be aware of issues that would make that integration difficult. When doing our preacquisition survey, we look for the ability to be self-aware, as well as a willingness to make changes midcourse if necessary.

TAKING STOCK OF VALUES

So, how do you find out if the company you are looking at matches up with you on the values front? Well, one way is to use a values survey like the one suggested in the sidebar, tweaked to focus on your particular company's concerns. Many of the most successful M&A firms add this type of survey to their financial and legal due diligence checklists to show that values are on an equal footing with more traditional aspects of the deal. Adding a values survey to your checklist will help you include this often-overlooked factor in M&A deals.

VALUES SURVEY

This survey can be used to help you articulate your own company's values, as well as be added to your traditional due diligence checklist.

Why was the company founded?

- What were the goals?
- Have they been accomplished?

What is the company's vision?

- What does the leadership want the organization to be?
- Are they achieving that?

What are the company's stated and implicit values?

- What is important to the organization?

How are decisions made?

- Is the approach hierarchical or collaborative?

How transparent is management?

- Does management let rank and file know why decisions are made?
- How do they ensure important information is shared throughout the organization?

What is the communication style?

- Are pronouncements top-down or are there more collaborative conversations?

How are employees treated?

- How are they expected to behave day-to-day?

How long do employees normally stay?

- Is there a lot of turnover?

How are desirable actions rewarded?

- How are undesirable actions discouraged?
- Is there an employee recognition program in place?

What is the approach to getting work done?

- Is the emphasis more on group collaboration or individual achievement?
- Do people pay more attention to methods or results?

What is the tolerance for risk?

- Are strategies more daring or conservative?

How is customer service done?

- What kinds of relationships are developed with customers?
- And how are complaints followed up on?

How do customers talk about the company?

- How do they interact with employees?

Is there more than one office?

- Is the culture consistent throughout all the offices?

How diverse is the executive team?

- And how do they ensure that commitment cascades down throughout the organization?

But it really starts with your CEO or founder getting along with the CEO or founder on the other side. If you understand what drives that person, then you can really get underneath what the company stands for. If I find somebody who is just looking to take the money and run, I might still do the deal, but I would do it in a much different way. I wouldn't depend on that person to drive the transaction or be part of the management going forward.

It takes more than a few emails or phone calls to get to know your counterpart. It takes unhurried, relaxed, in-person conversations. I will typically set up a meeting some place where we can just sit and talk uninterrupted for as long as we need to. You can never spend too much time with the founder or CEO. It is their values that trickle down through the organization. Once we are settled, I ask open-ended questions. Their answers are important, but maybe even more importantly, I want to know that they have an answer. So many people have never really thought about what drives their company. I want to know their thought processes. If all goes well, I'm going to be working with this CEO or founder and executive team for many years. I need to know we are compatible in our approach. Our leadership approaches don't need to be identical, but they can't be diametrically opposed. I'll ask why they founded the company or in the case of a hired CEO, why they are with the company. What is it about the company that they like? People who have been there a long time are there because there's something about that company they really relate to. If I get a chance, I'll ask some of the people on the exec team the same questions. If there is a disconnect in their answers, that would give me pause because everyone at the C-level should be pulling in the same direction.

You will probably never get a 100 percent understanding of everything that is involved in another firm's culture, but you need to understand enough that you feel comfortable to some level of satisfaction—80 percent, 85 percent, 90 percent, whatever your personal risk tolerance is—that their value sets are compatible and in sync with yours.

If they can't tell you why they're in business, what they stand for, or what they are trying to accomplish, then you need to think twice about going in and buying them. You can look them up on LinkedIn, you can know what schools they went to, you can know what other companies they have been part of, but you have no idea what they stand for. So why do people go ahead anyway? Often it's because the deal looks so good that they convince themselves that any culture or values mismatch can be worked out after the transaction closes.

NOT ALL DEALS ARE MEANT TO BE

A good example of a company talking itself into a deal that was never meant to be is the Proxicom / Dimensions Data transaction. Back in the late 1990s, Proxicom was a high-flying dot-com. It was one of the first companies in the web development space, and expanded quickly. By 2001, it had about seventeen hundred employees, nearly a dozen international offices, $148 million in net assets, and more than $200 million in revenues. However, like nearly all dot-coms of the time, it had never turned a profit. Also like nearly all dot-coms of the time, it saw its stock price crash when the dot-com bubble burst.

Despite tech volatility and the lack of profits, Proxicom found itself the subject of a bidding war between Compaq and South Africa–based Dimensions Data. Compaq bid $266 million for the fifty-eight million outstanding shares of Proxicom stock, and the bid was accepted. But then Dimensions Data came on the scene with a $422.2 million bid, and Proxicom quickly paid Compaq $10 million to nullify their contract and go away.

From the beginning this acquisition looked difficult. One company designed interactive websites, while the other developed hardware, such as routers and switches. One was a shiny American start-up, while the other was an established and staid South African manufacturer. There just didn't seem to be any synergies or areas to integrate. However, Dimensions Data believed this was their entry into the US market. If they got a bit of web development and consulting out of Proxicom, so much the better. As you would expect, the deal did not work out. Dimensions Data eventually sold Proxicom to an American private equity firm for less than $10 million in 2004. That was one of the most ill-conceived deals ever, and it was obviously so from the beginning. But the lure of being able to own one of the big names in interactive websites at what appeared at the time to be a bargain price was just too much to pass up. This was a case of a company wanting the deal to go through even if the due diligence didn't support it.

The thing to note here is that both companies were good at what they did. They just weren't good together. In fact, in 2008 iCrossing acquired Proxicom from a private equity firm because Proxicom's interactive websites were a good match for iCrossing's web-based search features. The cultures were similar. The management styles were similar. The products made sense together. This was a match made for success because we took the time to know what we were getting and developed a plan to integrate the company before the deal was finalized.

So how could Dimensions Data have avoided a failed transaction? By doing what I've been advocating in this chapter—meet with the founder or CEO of the other firm, and don't let yourself be swayed by wanting a deal to work. Some additional up-front interaction would have clearly pointed to the fact that the company was a proud organization. A successful organization like Proxicom would not want to serve as an up-front loss leader for hardware sales. It really made no sense.

When I was at iCrossing, a sole-proprietorship performance marketing firm in Buenos Aires caught my eye. We had been looking to expand into South America, and this firm looked like a perfect vehicle to do that. So, I made the trip to Buenos Aires to meet with the owner and make sure we were both on the same page. He welcomed me to his penthouse, and we had a lovely dinner. He seemed to have all the right answers. But as we began to do a credit check and look at the company financials, some things began to appear that didn't add up. In Brazil big ticket purchases need to be reported to the government for tax purposes. This fellow lived in a penthouse, had a luxury car, took exotic vacations— but according to government records, had never made a high-end purchase. As we dug further, we found that not only had he never reported a high-end purchase, he also hadn't ever paid taxes on the revenues of his very successful enterprise. Instead, he had funneled all of the money into shell corporations in Chile and Israel. When I asked him about the discrepancies, he was surprised that I was surprised. He told me that no one paid taxes in Brazil unless they had upset the authorities. We decided that even if these financial shenanigans were culturally OK in Brazil (and I have my doubts on that), this was one where our values were so at odds that we could never trust him or work with him.

I was disappointed this one didn't work out. On paper it was a great fit. But some deals are never meant to be. And you want to find out which ones those are before you sign the papers.

ALIGN YOUR COMMUNICATIONS PLAN

Many businesses make the mistake of creating a communications plan as they are about to seal the deal. This is a mistake. This needs to be done much earlier in the process. Once both parties feel committed to the acquisition, they need to figure out how they'll communicate the details to their respective companies, including the all-important role that values will play in the integration. Why? Because creating a plan forces you to articulate why you're undergoing a merger or acquisition in the first place—and to do that, you need to dig deeper into the reasons for making the agreement. In addition, you absolutely need to get your people, clients, and shareholders on board, or else the deal won't succeed. To do that, you need to help them see the deeper, cultural bonds that your two organizations share. Remember, we're living in a time when employees, clients, and shareholders are judging companies by their values. Set yourself up for success early on.

> **Remember, we're living in a time when employees, clients, and shareholders are judging companies by their values.**

When it comes time to execute your communications plan, you must own it (even if you hire someone to facilitate it). You can't delegate this job; it would be a big mistake. This is where your leadership comes into play. You are the messenger, cheerleader, and visionary all at once. You will likely be on the road, giving presentation after presentation, painting a picture of the future you see for the two companies. Your employees will want you to be the one to answer questions. Don't be surprised if someone asks a question you never thought to ask, despite spending months on the deal. But if the transaction has been built on shared values and missions, you should be able to intuit the answer because you know the other side so well. Over time your people will see the value that you see and you will be ready to begin the integration process, which we'll go into in the next few chapters.

ASK THE RIGHT QUESTIONS

Taking the time up front to assess an acquisition target's values and culture and make sure they align with yours can make all the difference between a successful acquisition deal and one that struggles. To assess those values, ask the right questions.

- Why is this transaction important to you? What value will it bring to your company—and the world?

- Do you believe our values and culture have similarities or align?

- At the deepest levels, what do you wish to accomplish?

- Why do you want to buy our company (or sell yours)? How will it expand your market reach?

- What do you think we can do for you? Can we help you sell new products to your existing clients?

These questions are not transactional; they are both strategic and extremely personal. M&A is all about the people. Take the time to get in sync with the values of the people on the other side of the table. If you fail to do this, you will run into problems down the integration road. Disagreements are typically caused by misaligned values. With proper alignment, however, the next stage of the process is more likely to proceed smoothly.

Businesses spend a lot of time comparing financial spreadsheets when they plan an acquisition. They need to share their values, mission, and vision too. Purpose, vision, and mission statements indicate where your two companies align—or don't. Likewise, assess the administrative or operational systems and processes to make sure they align with the mission statement, vision, and values. If gaps exist between the values and the mission and how they are expressed through the systems and processes, you risk working with a leader who doesn't walk the walk. If this is the case, there may still be reasons to continue with the transaction, but realize that caution and know that there will be substantial work to create alignment.

KEY TAKEAWAY

A lot of your success goes into how you plan up front. Take the necessary time to understand what you're buying. Learn to understand what motivates them. If you are all on the same page from the beginning, the rest is just sweating the details.

CASE STUDY

Hewlett Packard (HP) acquires Autonomy Corp.

Deal Size: $11.7 billion

Purpose: HP was looking to move into the software business

Outcome: HP took an $8.8 billion write-down a year later; Autonomy CFO was convicted of fraud

Autonomy was a software company founded in Cambridge, England, in 1996. By 2010, it had become the UK's largest software enterprise. In 2011 Autonomy was acquired by Hewlett-Packard, which was trying to quickly enter the high-margin software market. The deal valued

Autonomy at $11.7 billion, which was 79 percent over market value. Within a year HP had written off $8.8 billion of Autonomy's value, and in 2017 HP sold its Autonomy assets, as part of a wider deal, to the British software company Micro Focus.

So, what happened? In this case, it is almost easier to ask what didn't happen.

HP overpaid, which it also had done in previous acquisitions. The price paid raised eyebrows among analysts, reporters, and industry insiders. HP stock fell immediately after the deal was announced.

Autonomy's CFO was convicted of fraud and sent to jail for five years. Autonomy claimed that HP would have been able to uncover the fraudulent accounting had it done an adequate job of due diligence.

HP's CEO was replaced soon after the deal closed by Meg Whitman, who changed the management structure that Autonomy thought they were going to be part of. Autonomy's entire C-suite of executives left the company at that point.

And the high-flying entrepreneurial British software company simply clashed with the established US hardware company. Whitman was focused on bringing a relationship-based environment to HP, but Autonomy was a task-based, get-the-job-done place. HP had a calm, nonconfrontational culture, while Autonomy employees were used to a more confrontational workplace. Autonomy believed that HP had promised to let them continue to run their company independently. However, Autonomy employees came to feel that HP was imposing its processes, hierarchy, and collaborative meetings on them. Autonomy employees saw a relatively egalitarian structure become increasingly more hierarchical, which wasn't what they had signed up for.

SUCCESS OR FAILURE?

Overpaying for an acquisition does not in and of itself doom a deal to failure. It typically just means it will take longer to achieve profit and growth goals. Basing that too-good-to-be-true price on fraudulent financial numbers—which you didn't take the time to vet fully—would certainly be a blow, but again, not necessarily lethal. Autonomy was a very good company, with excellent revenue and growth potential, even if it wasn't as good as the fraudulent books indicated. But when the entire C-suite walks out and the rank and file feel they are being crushed from above, the ability to integrate the two entities is in real trouble. Despite all the chaos, this deal might have survived if HP had given Autonomy the autonomy they had been promised. In the end, it was better for both that they went their separate ways.

THE THICK OF IT (THE SLOG)

PART II

Take the time to make sure values and culture are aligned before you follow through on an acquisition. This gives both firms a better-than-average chance to succeed. To build a strong foundation is just the start. The real work begins when you integrate the two companies for the long term. The next two chapters will cover the importance of how to unify values from the very beginning, as well as to ensure that values drive everything you do.

CHAPTER FIVE

UNIFY VALUES IN YEAR ONE

nvestis, founded in 2000, made its mark by providing investor relations services for FTSE 250 companies in the UK before eventually branching into corporate communications. I was hired as CEO in North America in 2016, primarily to expand operations in the US. The US growth was slower than expected. This made me take a step back and start thinking about the strategy and business we were really in. We weren't in the investor relations business, and we weren't really in the corporate communications business either. We were in the content business because we were building, supporting, and supplying web content for our clients. This is the glue between all our products/ services. If you're going to develop content, then you want it to be found by the people whom you want to find it and you want them to find it when you want them to find it and on the device you want them to find it on. That all takes you into the area of performance marketing, in particular search engine optimization (SEO). It was my ah-ha moment. If we were in the digital content business, then we should be able to assist our clients with optimizing and amplifying such content, foundational skills of search engine optimization.

Once I convinced the board that's what we should do, I found a company in Arizona, ZOG Digital, that was in the SEO performance marketing business. It had the capabilities we needed, and its values and culture fit well with ours. We closed the deal, and we set about rebranding ZOG Digital and integrating it with Investis.

It was clear that trying to combine a twenty-year-old British company and a young, high-flyer tech company in Arizona would have its challenges.

To make sure everyone was on board with the rebranding, we involved teams from both companies and from each location. Rebranding involves lots of moving pieces, so we spent months weaving the process into the culture. One of the most important parts of any company's brand is its logo. A good logo connotes a company's products and character with one quick look. It's a tangible symbol for everyone in the company to rally around. We needed to get this part right.

I had a team in each of the offices—London, New York, and Phoenix—as well as an outside branding agency, Advantages, come up with a new logo for the company and present the design and its rationale to me and a steering committee. As we worked our way through this exercise, a lot of the discussion centered around what we stood for, how we wanted clients to view us, and how this could be represented in a logo.

investisdigital.

Investis digital logo

After everyone had presented, the Advantages design was far and away the best. It combined the two companies' names into Investis Digital and suggested a new color palette. The new logo and name brought everything together. In addition, because everyone on the leadership team had been part of coming up with a new design, it was almost instantly accepted by the people at both companies.

We spent a lot of time and effort integrating the new logo into signage, business cards, stationary, advertising, websites, and everywhere else a logo and corporate name would appear, but it was well worth it.

Why was the logo competition and rebranding so important? Because it gave the people at both companies the opportunity to have significant input into the new brand foundation and thus ensure a common rallying point as the new firm evolved. And it is the people that will make or break a deal. If you go into an acquisition thinking, "Well, we're bigger" or "We're smarter" or "We're just better" and expect the people at the acquired firm to just fall in line, you are setting yourself up for disaster. The firm you are buying was successful for a reason, and if you don't have an appreciation for that and work to transition in a way that captures the reasons that company was successful, you're going to fail for sure.

> **The firm you are buying was successful for a reason, and if you don't have an appreciation for that and work to transition in a way that captures the reasons that company was successful, you're going to fail for sure.**

Because we took the time to rebrand Investis and ZOG Digital into a new entity and because we embraced the strengths of both companies, no one was left feeling like an outsider. A rebranding is more than just a logo. The logo is the symbol, which represents the visual translation of the new brand foundation, but the rebranding work itself involves changing behavior and expectations. The essence of the new brand needs to permeate everything we do, and that takes time. As long as you engage your employees and work with them to rally around the new brand, your acquisition will increase your odds to be the one of the few that is able to succeed.

UNIFY AND ALIGN FROM YEAR ONE

An M&A deal takes anywhere from weeks to several months from start to finish. By the time the paperwork is signed, everyone is ready to breathe a sigh of relief and go back to just running the business. However, the real work has just begun. Be patient and expect the slog; the benefits are worth it. Although the deal has closed, the two companies still need to be integrated. Some people like to take things slow. They take a small step, then wait for everyone to become acclimated to that step. Then they take another small step. And so on. They feel it is easier to get used to change in small increments. In my experience this approach drags out the unification to a point that performance is often impacted because management, employees, and clients never feel settled. Just as they get used to one new process, another one is introduced.

Other companies like to just issue edicts from the top. "This is the way we have always done things, and this is the way the new company will do them as well." While this has some advantage in being quick, the disadvantages far outweigh its efficiency. Key people—and even not-so-key people—will undoubtedly make their displeasure at being overrun obvious by leaving. The people at the selling firm have done something right to make themselves an attractive acquisition. The buying firm needs to acknowledge that and work to find ways that processes and culture can be merged, as opposed to one simply being imposed on the other.

In my experience success comes when the goal is to unify around a purpose and values set as soon as possible, ideally within the first year, while still taking into account what each firm considers important to its own culture. This allows the new culture to evolve and reveal itself. It can take longer, but the longer it takes, the harder it will be to integrate the company. If the acquired company gets used to being an independent entity, it will be harder to pull it into the fold down the road.

Although it's not a common process, rebranding both companies is one of the best ways to unify the two entities. To rebrand at this stage makes it clear that everyone is now on equal footing within a new, unified vision and mission for the new company. This promotes loyalty in a way that being swallowed by a larger company and losing your corporate identity doesn't.

So, how do you rebrand or otherwise integrate an acquisition in a way that encourages management and employees to work together? The focus needs to be on leadership, communication, and respect.

PRIORITIZE LEADERSHIP PLUS COMMUNICATION AND RESPECT

Leadership is the first priority when an acquisition closes. The faster the top leadership team involved is established, the smoother the post-acquisition integration process will be. I usually put together a task force of people from both sides of the deal. We talk at least once a week, often more. We have a checklist of things that we developed in due diligence that we want to work through that includes how we're going to work together, how processes are going to flow through the system, how we're going to build common clients, how we're going to deliver an integrated/elevated/superior work product. All the process-related details that you need to nail down because if you don't, you not only look disjointed to employees and clients—you *are* disjointed.

I've mentioned before that values are all about people. There is no area where that is more evident than in retention of key personnel after a transaction has closed. During the due diligence process, you spend a fair amount of time reviewing the executive team, and maybe even the level below that. You get to know them pretty well, and you begin to make judgments on which ones will be driving the company going forward, which ones are at risk of leaving, and which ones might not have a place in the new organization. You can pretty much predict who is going to be there at the end and who is going to leave, but be prepared, there may be some surprises. There are always some people who simply don't like change, even change for the better, or feel the company is now moving in a direction they are uninterested in. Others might have been thinking about leaving even before the M&A transaction and simply see this as a good time to pull the trigger. However, your goal as a leader is to minimize those surprises. The success of the transaction is based on keeping the right people and putting them in the right roles. As mentioned in the HP/EDS acquisition case study, if the key people leave, the acquisition becomes a different company.

"Key man" contracts are often used to lock in crucial management execs. I've been on both sides of that one and have learned that it isn't incentives, compensation, or contracts that inspire loyalty. How you treat the people around you does. It's all a matter of respecting your people. When Hearst bought iCrossing, they gave me a good compensation and bonus package, but I also expected to be treated with some level of respect and be positioned as part of an executive team. Instead, they had me reporting to a middle-management manager. After that I knew that I would be leaving the minute I was contractually able to, whether they wanted me to stay or not.

When you are buying an asset, you certainly look at the products, capabilities, financials, and other tangible assets. But what you are really buying is the leadership team. That is where the value is. You know, I don't think you really realize how true that statement is until you see what can happen when the leadership team is ignored postclose. Assuming the company you are buying has been successful—and why would you buy an unsuccessful company?—it is the leadership team that has driven that success. It therefore makes sense to give that team the respect they deserve and do everything possible to integrate them into the new entity, where they can continue to drive success.

It is also up to the company's leadership to help employees understand the benefits of the acquisition. Employees often react negatively to the news of an acquisition because they don't know what to expect or what their place will be. Rumors thrive and spread in the vacuum created by a lack of official messaging. The leadership of successful acquisitions communicate as early as possible and as often as possible to employees, customers, partners, and the media. A vision must be clearly communicated to the new organization, with very clear lines on where the new company is going and how. Cisco Systems, which has acquired more than two hundred companies since 1993, has the integration process down to a science. It holds orientation sessions, makes regular company-wide updates, and is just generally transparent and open about the process. The company has even created a buddy system that pairs employees from the acquired company with counterparts at Cisco, so that they have someone to go to during the early days of the integration.

Recognizing that the company being acquired is made up of real live people who deserve respect and the courtesy of being kept in the loop on decisions that will affect their livelihoods will go a long way to smoothing the rough spots that occur in any transition.

While a company is focusing on integrating an acquisition, it can't lose sight of the fact that there is a business to run and clients to serve. However, it needs to make building its values-based foundation the priority. When Investis was integrating ZOG Digital, we didn't let the measurement system get in the way. Both companies were successful, and we didn't let the business slide, but we also didn't let ourselves be distracted by growth metrics. We weren't looking at what it would take to go from 22 percent growth to 28 percent growth. There was none of that discussion because we knew that we needed to integrate the firms first.

During the integration phase, it is not unusual for it to take a while to begin realizing the synergies and cost savings predicted by the due diligence that has been done. But the slow time should be limited to something like three to six months. As you come out of that period, you should see an acceleration in growth beyond where you would have been without the acquisition. The stronger the foundation you have built, the faster the growth will be. And the sooner you get that foundation built, the sooner you can get back to focusing on the business.

USING EARN-OUTS TO ALIGN MANAGEMENT

Earn-outs are a common method to bridge the gap between what the purchasing firm thinks the seller is worth and what the seller thinks it is worth, as well as to align the leadership of the new firm with the old. Typically, an earn-out allows the principals at the selling company to remain for a period of time, usually one to three years, though it can be longer. If the seller reaches certain performance milestones during that time, then the acquirer will make additional payments.

On paper, the earn-out-style transaction looks like a good way to solve the problem of an entrepreneur who has overvalued his or her company, as well as align leadership teams because everyone is shooting for the same goals and trying to get to the same targets.

In reality, earn-outs create disincentives because of all the things you have to do to protect the earn-out. The nature of the transaction encourages the acquirer to leave the selling firm alone until the earn-out period ends. The selling firm will make the argument that it cannot be expected to reach the earn-out hurdles if it is required to change its name, processes, reporting structure, personnel, compensation, and other things that typically go with being bought out.

On the other hand, the buyer has no real incentive to help the seller reach the earn-out goals since it will increase the price of the selling firm and require the buying firm to make additional payments.

This setup makes it difficult, if not impossible, to integrate the two firms. The acquired company in essence becomes a wholly owned subsidiary or independent division. If that was the goal from the beginning, then fine. You've achieved it. But if the idea was to fully integrate the two firms under one umbrella with shared values and branding, then you have set yourself up for a long, difficult process. You won't really be able to begin integrating until the earn-out period ends, and by that time, the management and employees of the selling firm have grown used to their independence. Changing the playing field at that time can be done, but it will be more difficult than if you had been able to integrate everyone at the very beginning. An earn-out transaction is the antithesis of successful integration and the creation of new shared values.

Despite the downside of earn-outs, they are ubiquitous in the professional services industry. That means that you will likely find yourself involved in an earn-out transaction at some time. That also means that in such cases surveying the values and culture of the company you are dealing with before the paperwork is signed is more important than ever. You are not going to have the chance to mold, adjust, or interweave values to form a new foundation to form a new company—at least not for a couple of years. So, it is imperative that the values match from the beginning. At least you will know that you align on the important things, even if your two firms act in parallel for a while.

The acquisition process does not stop when the last signature on the closing papers is notarized. In fact, then the hard work begins. No matter how diligent you are in choosing a company with the right capabilities, leadership, and values, integrating two companies is always a challenge. One way to avoid the roadblocks incurred by teams feeling like outsiders is to rebrand the two companies, so you start with a brand-new entity encompassing the best processes, features, values, and culture of the buying and selling firms.

Two years or so after an acquisition, you should not be able to tell which employees and executive team members came from the acquired firm and which ones were with the buying firm. If everyone pulls together as one entity and performance has met the acquisition goals, then that is what success looks like.

KEY TAKEAWAY

Anyone involved in the professional services industry will likely be part of a merger or acquisition at some point. As a leader, it will be up to you to actually lead the communication with your team and that of your counterpart and work to integrate the values of the two firms based on mutual respect, purpose, and vision for the combined entity.

CASE STUDY

Microsoft acquires aQuantive

Deal Size: $6.3 billion

Purpose: Microsoft expects to use aQuantive's capacities to build an online advertising business and become a viable rival to Google

Outcome: Microsoft wrote off $6.2 billion five years later

In 2007 Microsoft purchased Seattle-based aQuantive—a display advertising software firm with twenty-six hundred employees and rapidly growing profits and revenue—for $6.3 billion, the largest acquisition it had ever made. Microsoft's goal was to quickly get a foothold in the digital advertising space and compete with Google. Five years later Microsoft had lost $10.4 billion on its online services, and the bloom was off the aQuantive rose. The company took a $6.2 billion goodwill write-off, primarily because of its aQuantive acquisition.

What went wrong? Analysts point to several missteps, including Microsoft's insistence on focusing on search rather than display advertising, despite the fact that aQuantive was a display advertising firm. But in the long run—or short run, as the case may be—much of the failure can be attributed to a culture clash. It became increasingly difficult to combine the engineering-centric culture of Microsoft with the advertising-centric mindset of aQuantive.

One aQuantive executive is quoted in GeekWire as explaining, "The task of evangelizing the business of advertising—not software—was akin to asking Willie Wonka to grow vegetables. No amount of explanation about ad revenue versus software revenue or Google's plan to make software free could refocus a Windows-obsessed culture.

As far as online advertising was concerned, the more important and familiar task was building a better search algorithm. Period."

Microsoft's culture made it hard to integrate online services, which require more frequent product releases and constant contact with customers. The long product cycles of Windows create a much different development model

SUCCESS OR FAILURE?

The Microsoft/aQuantive deal ran into the problem endemic in the acquisition of smaller, nimble software companies by larger, established firms. Microsoft recognized the benefits of aQuantive's software products but didn't know what to do with the people once it had the company. Although aQuantive was allowed relative operational independence, being required to conform to Microsoft's focus on search rather than display ads destroyed its mojo.

CHAPTER SIX

BRING VALUES TO LIFE

Today's employees and clients want to know what you stand for and what you believe in. It is no longer enough to work with a firm that offers excellent services; clients want to work with firms that align with them on beliefs and values. Customers demand more than a transaction; they want conversation and collaboration that evokes feelings. And employees want leaders who lead, who know what they and the company stand for and help the corporate culture conform to that vision.

So how do you live your corporate values and communicate them to your employees and clients? In every way you can.

Investis commercial

Soon after Investis and ZOG Digital combined and the new Investis Digital was formed, we did a video of an elevator pitch to let everyone inside and outside the company know what we did and what we stood for.[6] I didn't want to just stand in front of the camera and spout words from a prepared script. I wanted the words to actually mean something. I wanted to make sure the viewers not only heard what we stood for but saw and felt it as well.

By definition, an elevator pitch should be in an elevator, which meant we needed to find a working elevator that no one was using. After following several false leads, our creative team found a nearly completed building that had a safe, functioning elevator but no tenants yet. We made a deal with the owner to rent the building for the day, and we set about filming our video. The camera follows me from the time I enter the elevator until I get off at my floor, all the while answering questions about the company as more people enter the elevator at each stop. By the time I get off, all of the people in the elevator know exactly what we stand for, as do the viewers.

---

6   You can see the elevator pitch video here: https://vimeo.com/290901607.

The questions and answers in the video are certainly important in getting our point across, but just as important are the visuals—it's a video, not a podcast, after all. The people entering the elevator range from office workers and delivery people to doctors and soldiers, from cooks and police to rabbis and even Elmo. It's a collection of people (and Muppets) that subtly drives home the point that Investis Digital is the right company and has the right products for a wide variety of customers. We provide cutting-edge solutions, but we don't take ourselves too seriously. As I talk about our values and what we do, the video intersperses clips showing how our people spend their days at work and actually do the things I'm talking about—how they implement our values in everything they do. The visuals bring my words to life, and the viewers see for themselves, experiencing the passion and innovation that makes the company what it is.

The video was recognized by the industry and won several awards for its content and was viewed thousands of times online by our team, our clients, and the world. It got to the point quickly where clients would tell us they'd seen the video and how much it resonated with them. They valued the information it was meant to communicate and how it was conveyed. The reason the video was such a hit wasn't just that it was well crafted—which it was—but that it was authentic. Viewers could hear, see, and feel the "real" Investis Digital. It wasn't just an international public relations spin. It was genuine—and the viewers felt it.

BE YOURSELF

In an age of scripted reality shows, alternative facts, and social media "friends" you've never met, to be authentic can differentiate your company from others.

We've all known people or companies who say one thing and do another. Customers are way smarter today at sniffing out the disconnect. Unfortunately, that behavior is so common that when companies like Nordstrom or Trader Joe's stand behind their products with "no questions asked" return policies, it is unusual enough to become the stuff legends are made of. The Nordstroms and Trader Joe's of the world really shouldn't be such a rarity because being authentic is simply good business practice. It is actually easier and more productive than just giving lip service to ideals. If what you are doing is rooted on a set of shared values, everything else will flow naturally. There won't be a lot of time wasted on "should I do this or should I do that?" Different teams within the organization won't be at odds because they will all be empowered to work from the same shared values set. Problem-solving won't get bogged down in a myriad of possible solutions. The right answer will be the one that fits your company's values. You will also have more time to do what you need to because you empowered your team to use those values as a guide of "what to do" rather than come to you to make decisions.

An attractive target firm will more often than not be choosing from among several suitors. And the deciding factors are often the intangibles, such as trust.

Having a reputation for being an organization that means what it says and stands behind its promises is important when it comes to finding willing acquisition targets. Not every company is actively selling itself when it is approached by a potential buyer. They sometimes have to be convinced that this is a good deal for both parties. And often, good firms have choices. An attractive target firm will more often than not be choosing from among several suitors. And the deciding factors are often the intangibles, such as trust.

I cannot tell you how many times an acquired company CEO has told me that we were not the highest price offered but they took our offer because we were the right one. It was because we were authentic to ourselves and we acted that way. They were comfortable and believed we would live up to our word. These types of endorsements are invaluable and stand the test of time.

During the transaction process, both firms have to trust that the other is being authentic. We can look at financial statements and sign legal documents, but we need to trust that the other party means what they say when it comes to execution. You don't want to end up with the CEO of the acquired firm walking out the door on the first day—unless that had been agreed to earlier. And the acquired firm doesn't want to suddenly find the majority of its people considered redundant—unless that had been agreed to earlier. No amount of paperwork will keep bad actors from acting badly. It's simply in their nature. Conversely, no amount of paperwork is needed for authentic actors to act authentically. It's simply in their nature.

If your company is based on a strong set of values, then to be authentic will come naturally, and it will improve your chances of acquiring the firms you want to acquire. To be authentic preclose helps the target company feel at ease that you are real and not just telling them what they want to hear prior to close. Being authentic postclose gives everyone reassurance that you are a person of your word and you will live up to promises made. Being authentic is simply good business practice.

LIVE YOUR VALUES

When we talk about values and ideals, we talk about what your individual company stands for. One company's values are not necessarily better than another's. For example, some companies might value social activism, while others prefer that employees concentrate on their jobs. Some might value collaboration, while others value individual contributions. Some are risk-averse, while others swing for the fences. No matter what your shared values are, however, you need to communicate them clearly and often to your employees.

For example, the founder and CEO of the cryptocurrency firm Coinbase once wrote a blog post that clarified his company's mission and values. The company had experienced a virtual walkout by employees upset that the founder hadn't gotten behind a particular social justice movement. The CEO affirmed that he personally supported the movement but it was not part of the company's mission or culture to become involved in outside causes. He wanted the company's culture to be apolitical and laser-focused on moving the company forward. His blog post outlined the culture he wanted to instill and listed values that supported that culture. But he went further. He provided very clear examples of what, as a company, Coinbase would and would not do:

We focus on the things that help us achieve our mission:

- **Build great products:** The vast majority of the impact we have will be from the products we create, which are used by millions of people.

- **Source amazing talent:** We create job opportunities for top people, including those from underrepresented backgrounds who don't have equal access to opportunities, with things like diverse slates (Rooney rule) on senior hires, and casting a wide net to find top talent.

- **Fair talent practices:** We work to reduce unconscious bias in interviews, using things like structured interviews, and ensure fair practices in how we pay and promote. We have a pay for performance culture, which means that your rewards and promotions are linked to your overall contribution to the mission and company goals.

- **Enable belonging for everyone:** We work to create an environment where everyone is welcome and can do their best work, regardless of background, sexual orientation, race, gender, age, etc.

We focus minimally on causes not directly related to the mission:

- **Policy decisions:** If there is a bill introduced around crypto, we may engage here, but we normally wouldn't engage in policy decisions around healthcare or education for example.

- **Nonprofit work:** We will do some work here with our Pledge 1% program and GiveCrypto.org, but this is about 1% of our efforts. We are a for-profit business. When we make profit, we can use that to hire more great people, and build even more. We shouldn't ever shy away from making profit, because with more resources we can have a greater impact on the world.

- **Broader societal issues:** We don't engage here when issues are unrelated to our core mission, because we believe impact only comes with focus.

- **Political causes:** We don't advocate for any particular causes or candidates internally that are unrelated to our mission, because it is a distraction from our mission. Even if we all agree something is a problem, we may not all agree on the solution.

The values statement was communicated to the employees via a blog, an email, and a company town hall.

The point here isn't that a nonactivist company is better or more profitable than an activist company. It's that the Coinbase CEO has a very clear idea of what values he wants the company to stand on, and he is very clear on how they should be implemented. He is making sure that the company's values flow through everything it does.

And that's the whole point. It doesn't do any good to have a values-based company if you aren't embracing those values in everything you do.

HOW TO DO IT

In an ideal world, everyone would just intuit a company's values from its actions. But we don't live in an ideal world, so it's important to proactively reference the values every time you can. Embracing your values isn't a "nice to do" but rather a "must-do" if you want your business and acquisitions to succeed.

Let's take Investis Digital's values[7] as an example, starting with "Embrace Clarity." Clarity is all about clear communication. We avoid using technical jargon. We keep all of our emails, proposals, and other communications simple. This is actually a cost- and time-efficient way to communicate. When you keep things simple, you reduce the chances of being misunderstood. Studies have shown that poor communication results in higher turnover and employee absenteeism. One survey conducted by the Computing Technology Industry Association involving one thousand computer professionals found that poor communication was considered to be the main cause of failure to deliver

---

7   You can view the Investis Digital Culture video here: https://vimeo.com/300082396.

a project within its agreed upon time frame.[8] To embrace clarity is simply good business practice.

Investis office

Our second value is "Bring Passion." We expect our employees to bring their best every day. We are a collaborative company, with employees who go over and above to help their teams and customers. They do it not because they have seen a line item on the "Values" board that says, "Bring Passion." They do it because they truly enjoy their jobs and they are committed to customer success. We've created a culture that allows these emotions to flourish.

Our "Inspire Greatness" value is one that flows through every part of the company. We aren't looking for Nobel Prize winners—although we wouldn't mind having one. We are looking for people who do their jobs in such a way that others want to emulate them. Maybe the office manager knows the name of everyone in the company, as well as every client and their assistants, delivery people, cleaning staff,

---

8   Linda Rosencrance, "Survey: Poor communication causes most IT project failures," Computerworld, March 9, 2007, https://www.computerworld.com/article/2543770/ survey--poor-communication-causes-most-it-project-failures.html#:~:text=Poor communication is the reason,-based trade association

and corporate board members. Taking the time to learn someone's name when they call or stop by never fails to make them feel special. Maybe it's a team lead who goes out of their way to mentor and listen to the ideas of the youngest and most inexperienced team members. Maybe it's someone from the marketing team who reviews the presentations of every keynote speaker and leading panelist in the industry. Whatever the role, it can be done in a way that inspires others to greatness—you just need to recognize what's needed for the employee or team member to accomplish this. Encourage them and acknowledge progress.

Our fourth value is that of "Constant Innovation," an important value to our company for sure. We constantly seek out new trends and innovations because being the best means constantly innovating. Companies that rest on their laurels soon find themselves passed up by a younger, hungrier competitor. There is always one more thing to learn, one more problem to solve, one more challenge to master.

Finally, we measure success. Without metrics, how do you know you've succeeded? A gut feel isn't good enough. How often have you heard a salesperson come out of a meeting and declare, "That was a great meeting! We really connected. She told me about a new restaurant in town that I need to try." But when you ask how the meeting brought them closer to a sale, they can't tell you. They have no metrics to base the apparent success of the meeting on. We measure everything we do. That's our responsibility as a trusted partner. By implementing objective metrics, we know if we are providing the innovative solutions our clients expect.

I've been talking about each shared individual value, but values are not discrete. They are Intertwined. The team with the leader who is passionate and inspires greatness is always innovating. The clear proposal that outlines the specific metrics that will be used to measure success provides an innovative solution. When everyone in the company is embracing the corporate values, they don't need to think about them. They simply act in a way that promotes the mission of the company.

RECOGNIZING VALUE-DRIVEN BEHAVIOR

People don't do well in a vacuum. They need air to breathe. When we are talking about encouraging behavior based on corporate values, that air is recognition. One of the ways we recognize those who live our corporate values in everything they do is through the Donnie Awards.

The Donnie Awards are presented during a company event that is live cast to all of our offices each year around the same time as the Oscars. There are five categories to mirror our five value statements, and three divisions within each category—Team, Individual, and Project. People within the company nominate those they believe have best epitomized a particular value during the year. Last year we had something like 175 nominations. Those nominations go through a vetting process, and we choose several semifinalists. I then choose a winner. When the winner is announced at the ceremony, the video feed cuts to whichever office they are in, and we make a big deal of presenting them with a trophy. After we award the trophy, the winners are interviewed "backstage" the same way Oscar winners are. The trophy is theirs and will sit on their desk for as long as they work with us. It lets everyone know that the efforts of this person are remarkable and are being recognized by the entire company. We want these employees to inspire greatness in their peers. And we want them to know that we recognize what they have done for the company.

The Donnie Awards are the highlight of our year, but we don't wait for one huge gala to let people know that we notice when they embrace our values. Our communications plan is very intentional. It includes ways to make sure we stress the values in everything we do and highlights ways we see them being implemented. For example, if somebody delivers fantastic project work for a client, we will cite that in a company-wide communication called Don's Download and note the values it encompasses. I might also note it in one of my blog posts. When we cite tangible examples of the values in action, others within the organization see and feel exactly how those values underpin and impact everything we do. We keep ourselves on high alert. We also look for ways to keep our teams engaged. For example, in the work-from-home days during the pandemic, we had a contest to choose the best at-home setup. This activity let our employees know that we value them and helped everyone stay engaged and passionate about their work.

VALUES AND YOUR ACQUISITIONS

At this point, you might ask, what does all of this has to do with the acquisition process? I'd respond that it might not seem like it has a lot to do with a conventional acquisition process, but you would see me sit up in my chair, look you straight into your eyes, and say, "When you embrace your values in everything you do, the values become second nature." They're naturally authentic. It's not unusual for a company that espouses transparency to assure everyone that they won't interfere with the acquired company's operations and culture, only to turn around and impose new requirements and processes. Employees and management at the acquired company become disenchanted and soon leave. The acquiring firm is left with nothing but a shell of the company it thought it was buying. Promises made but not kept lead to significant issues later on.

One of the case studies I included earlier in this book looked at Hearst's acquisition of iCrossing. Lots of promises were made, primarily focused on how Hearst was going to use its network of sales-people and current clients to increase iCrossing's revenues. This didn't happen. In fact, the Hearst teams were actively discouraged from helping their iCrossing counterparts. Instead of viewing the iCrossing team as part of the organization, they saw them as competition for sales. It should have been no surprise to anyone that iCrossing soon experienced an exodus of key—and not so key—people. The company has never recovered its mojo. And it was all because iCrossing relied on promises made when it was being courted but not kept once the deal was consummated.

If you know in advance which values are important to you, it can save a lot of time when talking to your counterpart at the target company. You may see some things in their shared values that are different than your own value sets. Those are the things that can get you in trouble later. Proceed with caution; it can save you thousands of dollars and hours of time. Take the time to talk them out before the deal closes. This won't be something you can fix later, easily, or cheaply. "OK, I understand this value is important to your company. How does that manifest itself? Is that going to be an issue if the combined entity isn't grounded on that value?" But that talk can only happen if you are very clear on your own values. If they are running through everything your company does, you can't help but be clear.

When you look to buy a company, it's not just the employees who need to be comfortable with the combined entity. The current and future clients are equally as important. To avoid losing clients, both companies should be on the same page so that they can present a united front. We have two- to three-day client summits every year, where we bring our most engaged clients together for several days of expert presentations, bonding, and client networking. Clients are smart and can see through a company that is just pretending to be customer-first or innovative or whatever the shared value is. They can also sense rather quickly when there is "trouble in paradise" with your newest acquisition. Our goal is to work with our own clients, as well as build trust with the acquisition firm's clients. We help them communicate authentically with the people they do business with, no matter where they are in the digital space. We can't do that if we aren't authentic ourselves.

> **A shared value set needs to underpin everything your company does.**

A shared value set needs to underpin everything your company does. How do you know if you've succeeded in promoting your values? Ask your employees. Can they name the values? How do they impact their day-to-day job? Ask your clients. How would they describe your company? Ideally, both employees and clients will reference the same values.

KEY TAKEAWAY

You do not want one set of values that underpins corporate operations and another that is brought into play only for mergers or acquisitions. If you have an authentic, values-based company, the same values that build trust with clients will serve you well when it comes to executing an acquisition transaction.

CASE STUDY

Sapient acquires Nitro Group

Deal Size: $50 million in cash and stock

Goal: To add traditional advertising capabilities

Outcome: Acquisition succeeded in providing both companies with additional capabilities

---

In 2009 digital marketing firm Sapient Corp. acquired Nitro Group in a deal valued at $50 million. What made this deal so interesting was that it was the digital agency acquiring the traditional advertising agency. Nearly all of the other agency acquisitions at this time had involved traditional agencies adding digital capabilities. Now the recession was turning the tables as clients wanted to save on costs by having a one-stop shop. If Sapient wanted to continue to acquire large clients and differentiate itself from its digital competitors, it was going to have to offer them both digital and traditional services.

Sapient spent close to a year looking for the right partner. During this time Sapient approached several large, well-known agencies such as W&K and Modernista! However, according to Sapient Interactive's worldwide creative officer at the time, Gaston Legorburu, it was Nitro's Asia Pacific strength, coupled with its culture, that made it more attractive than the better-known agencies. "There were great agencies we talked to, where I was in awe of the level of creativity, but we were not going to be able to live together," he said. "We were very careful in terms of aligning with an agency that fit."

Despite Sapient claiming they were looking for a cultural fit, outsiders had their doubts. Sapient was an engineer-based company with a reputation for rules and processes. Nitro was freewheeling and creative. It was hard to see how the two cultures would mesh.

However, both companies had a strong incentive to make it work. They needed each other if they were to differentiate themselves from their larger, better-known, better-financed competitors. The trick would be to balance their strengths. Sapient needed to be careful that it kept its credibility with its high-end digital consultancy clients, while Nitro needed to make sure it didn't lose the creative edge that attracted Sapient. It could easily turn out to be a war between the artists and the engineers.

During the next two years, Sapient rebranded Nitro into Sapient-Nitro and set it up as a separate agency arm. Nitro's founder and CEO left to start a new company, stating that he was an entrepreneur at heart and couldn't pass up the chance to be part of a new start-up. And the companies settled into a very successful partnership.

In the past ten years, the Sapient / Nitro acquisition has proven to be the start of a very good growth trend. At the time of the acquisition, Sapient had revenues of about $690 million. In 2015 the French marketing group Publicis Groupe acquired Sapient for $3.7 billion. Soon after that acquisition, the SapientNitro division was merged with Publicis's digital group, Razorfish, to become SapientRazorfish. In 2019 Sapient Consulting and SapientRazorfish were merged into one brand, Publicis Sapient.

SUCCESS OR FAILURE?

This acquisition could have easily turned into a "fail" story. But Sapient's awareness of looking for a cultural fit from the beginning was key to making it work. While the two firms appeared to have competing cultures, Sapient was able to sidestep that hurdle by setting up Nitro as its own division. Both groups were able to live happily under one roof, if in different rooms. Neither group tried to impose its culture on the other and, instead, looked for what united them rather than separated them. It probably helped that the market moved to a "digital first" emphasis, which allowed the dominant firm, Sapient, to maintain its dominance in the structure, but bottom line— both companies were aware of the importance of respecting each other's culture and worked to maintain the strengths their cultures brought to the deal.

VALUE THAT WILL LAST

PART III

Getting an acquisition across the finish line is hard work. It usually takes many months to source an attractive acquisition target, connect with the executive team to determine if the two companies can play well together, work through the financial and legal diligence, and smooth all the inevitable bumps in the road that occur along the way. Once those final papers are signed, it's no wonder that many companies think their work is done. The leadership team has spent hundreds of hours working on the deal, which has taken time away from their day-to-day activities. Everyone is anxious to get back to their normal routines. In reality they are only about half done. They've completed the deal. Now they need to integrate the new company to create lasting value. It's at this stage that leadership will make the difference between a successful acquisition and one that is talked about as a "lesson learned."

CHAPTER SEVEN

MAKE IT LAST

C losing an acquisition is just the beginning. The hard part is integrating two organizations. This is where leadership can make all the difference.

In the previous chapter, I explained how we integrated ZOG Digital with Investis to form Investis Digital, but that was really just half the story—because it was just half of the transaction. We didn't just buy ZOG Digital—we bought a second company, Vertical Measures, within a year.

In 2016 Investis was at a crossroads. It was always seen as an investor relations and communications company, but after being in business for sixteen years, growth opportunities looked to be slowing. I was brought in to turn around the situation in the US, and one of the first things I did was help the board understand the need to pivot from the company's historical roots to acknowledging and embracing what it was actually doing now—providing digital content. To ramp up our digital communications capabilities, we determined that we needed to assist our clients in optimizing and amplifying their content through techniques like search engine optimization (SEO). As a result we began to look for a company that had world-class capabilities in SEO and would make an immediate impact for us. A bold move for our company, and one that was truly strategic.

This led us to ZOG Digital. This was an important transaction. We were looking to ZOG Digital to facilitate Investis's change in direction and strategy. It was crucial we did it right and made it last because we weren't just adding capabilities to our platform, we were also about to pivot to create a new foundation. But an acquisition wouldn't be an acquisition if everything went smoothly.

The due diligence and closing were relatively painless, with minimal preclose issues, but soon after we closed, a couple of issues popped up that caused us serious concern. When we developed the business plan for Investis plus ZOG Digital, we expected to see a combined growth rate of about 30 percent the first year. ZOG Digital was on a trajectory to grow 20 percent before the acquisition, and we thought Investis could contribute an additional 10 percent in cross-sell opportunities. However, within the first six months, ZOG Digital lost two large clients, which represented more than 10 percent of the company's revenues. In this business, clients churn for a variety of reasons, but in this case the timing could not have been worse. The whole economic case was based on both companies continuing on their growth trajectories. After losing those clients in the first six months, it appeared growth would be much slower than anticipated.

Despite this setback, the justification for the acquisition was still valid. It was important to stay focused on why we had acquired ZOG

Digital and work to right the ship. It was my responsibility to keep us focused. Maintaining stability would prove to be so important later on.

We all knew we needed to replace that lost revenue, so we spent significant time educating our sales force on the advantages that ZOG brought, as well as explaining the purpose of the acquisition to our current clients. During these early months, we also had some turnover at the staff level, but that is something that is expected during any acquisition and can be planned for. The ZOG founder also left. This had been expected as well, but it meant that we lost a valuable link to the company's current clients and pipeline. Although things started off a bit rocky, within nine months we had picked up enough new clients and additional business from current clients to get us back on track. While we hadn't done anything spectacular to get to this point, it was the focus that charted the path to calm. To some it looked like we just took care of business and didn't panic. That is my responsibility as CEO, and I owned it. We focused on what we needed most—sales— and made sure that everyone knew the fundamental reasons for the acquisition were still solid. Leadership projected an air of confidence that kept everyone on track to make it work. And it did.

A year after buying ZOG Digital, another acquisition opportunity, Vertical Measures, came along that added a significant new boost to our ZOG Digital transaction. This was a "bolt-on" acquisition, which basically means you are buying a company that does something you already do. You're simply "bolting on" additional capabilities. The acquired company is not adding anything significantly new to your product suite but is adding additional capabilities of doing essentially the same thing. The additional capability allows you to deliver more and, theoretically, capture a larger market share.

The integration of Vertical Measures was much smoother than that of ZOG Digital, primarily because the founder of Vertical

Measures stayed with us for an extended period and was invested in making sure the deal worked. From the beginning he used his relationships with his clients to make them comfortable with the changes, so none left. He focused on his sales pipeline so that none of the prospects fell through the cracks. Vertical Measures' preclosing growth trajectory had been 20 percent, just as ZOG Digital's had been. However, having the founder working as hard to make the integration work as he had to build the company in the first place made all the difference.

What sets these two acquisitions apart from the standard acquisition story is a little quirk of geography. A few months after we acquired ZOG Digital, the founder of Vertical Measures reached out to me to see if we would be interested in acquiring his firm. He was very well acquainted with ZOG Digital and had been impressed with the acquisition process. He knew ZOG so well because not only were they both located in Scottsdale, AZ, but they were also both in the same building, just one floor apart. The integration meetings simply involved getting off the elevator one floor earlier or later, depending on whom I was going to see.

While the proximity of the two firms made corporate visits easy, it also had an unexpected downside. It turned out the two founders were competitive and didn't really get along that well. One, in particular, went out of his way to irritate the other. Spending their days just an elevator ride away from each other gave them more than the normal number of interactions to stoke their animosity. For example, one CEO paid extra to have his firm's signage placed just outside the window of the other, so his rival CEO would have to look at it every time he opened his curtains. They were both friendly, likable people in their own right but were just oil and water when put together. This feud could have complicated the integration of the two companies, but both founders wanted to leave relatively soon after the closing, so that potential problem fell to our leadership team to manage through.

Performance marketing is a small industry, and it's even smaller when you are talking about one city. Everybody knows everybody, and many of the employees had, at one time or another, worked for the rival firm. This meant that the cultures and values at the two firms were very similar. Once the two leaders were gone, the firms were combined. Both moved onto the same floor in their shared building and then were rebranded with Investis as Investis Digital.

You can contrast the result of these acquisitions with the Hearst acquisition of iCrossing that we talked about at the beginning of the book. There, you had a print company buying an online company. On paper, it all should have worked. However, when iCrossing began to lose customers, Hearst had no idea what to do. Unlike Investis, which doubled down on helping ZOG Digital replace its lost clients, Hearst simply wasn't invested in promoting its new iCrossing asset. As clients began to leave, top iCrossing staff soon followed. There was a downward spiral from there, and iCrossing never recovered. It's been ten years since Hearst acquired iCrossing, and the digital company is less than half its former size.

The difference in outcomes between the Hearst/iCrossing acquisition and the Investis / ZOG Digital / Vertical Measures transactions can be directly traced to alignment of leadership and the companies' shared values along with clear objectives—or lack thereof.

LEADERSHIP IS KEY

Every M&A will cause upheaval within the companies involved. Change, even good change, is always hard. As the leader of the transaction, a CEO must integrate the firms and connect all the employees by showing them what will be achieved together and how it is much greater than what could be achieved separately. Without strong, effective leadership, the chances that a transaction will reach its full potential are small.

What makes a good leader, however, is a subject that is debated in a multitude of articles, blogs, research studies, and books. Universally accepted best practices for leading are difficult to define because we are dealing with people. What motivates one person will turn off another. What one employee views as reasonable and fair will cause another to run to HR. Different business situations call for different styles of leadership. All of that being said, I have found four core aspects of leadership have helped me successfully integrate multiple companies that create lasting value.

Have a Plan

I think Lewis Carroll put it best: "If you don't know where you are going, any road will get you there." Before anything is signed, both leadership teams should agree to a business plan that outlines in detail how the new company is going to get from here to there. The plan will include a forecast for growth that takes into account each company's strengths, weaknesses, and capabilities and provides a blueprint of how the two can be most effectively combined. It is at this stage that redundant personnel and operations become evident, and plans should be made for how those redundancies will be handled. The plan should also include activities that blend the teams and incentives that encourage the teams to work together. It's natural for teams from each company to be protective of their products, processes, and culture. You'll need to work hard to lead with intention to break down the barriers.

Be Decisive

Good leaders take into account the ideas and opinions of those around them. They want to make sure that stakeholders feel heard and valued. Seeking different perspectives allows the leader to grasp emerging trends and understand what to consider most important. But in the end, the leader must make the decision and ensure it is executed. Some decisions are harder than others. Letting someone go because they no longer fit the organization is always hard but so is making a decision when there are two viable alternatives. Once the decision is made, the leader needs to project certainty so that others in the organization feel comfortable following.

Prioritize Results

Leaders with a strong results orientation tend to emphasize the importance of efficiency and productivity and to prioritize the highest-value work. Decisions are based on data and measurable metrics. This style of leadership not only drives growth effectively, but it also provides an atmosphere of fairness and consistency because, transparently, everyone can understand how the decision was made.

Overcommunicate

Communication is key before, during, and after the transition. Don't leave your employees and staff in the dark. As soon as you can, let them know what is happening and how it will affect them. You want to control the narrative so it doesn't control you. Get ahead of gossip and rumors.

To make sure nothing gets missed, create a formal communications plan. The plan should outline how you are going to clearly communicate the "why" behind the acquisition. Explain the positive impacts the transaction will have. Clients are the most important nonemployee stakeholder to address. Some clients may say they preferred the original smaller firm and may leave. Many other clients, however, will be excited to have access to the increased capabilities. Every communication related to the acquisition should remind your employees, your clients, and the leaders of the merging entities about the purpose, values, and story of the new business.

> To make sure nothing gets missed, create a formal communications plan. The plan should outline how you are going to clearly communicate the "why" behind the acquisition.

Just as important as communicating the positive outcomes of the acquisition is acknowledging the negatives. You don't need to dwell on the fact that the acquired company headquarters will be moving or that some roles will be eliminated, but you shouldn't ignore them either. Employees and customers will trust you more if they believe you are telling them the whole truth and not hiding the harder realities. When you communicate the negative news, outline how the company is going to mitigate the effects. Building and keeping trust is important during any transition. It is even more important when a company is being bought and potentially losing its identity.

A McKinsey research report does a good job of outlining the objectives of a good communications plan.[9]

- Focus on business objectives. This is the opportunity to define your purpose and share your new story in the market.

- Start early and tailor. Messages should address the stakeholders' evolving needs. If you cannot communicate decisions yet, explain the process.

- Communicate your values. If, for example, bottom-up thinking is part of the new shared values set, top-down messaging will not align.

- Be consistent and compelling. This is your story! The more compelling it is, the more successful it will be. All communication should be of high quality and repeatedly reinforced in multiple channels. Communicate five times more than you think you need to.

- Humanize the message. Address what people really care about in a tone that is responsive to the mood and situation, not overly formal and legalistic. Shared values do not communicate well in legalese.

- Empower your leaders. Actively align leaders, middle managers, and customer-facing staff so that they communicate effectively and consistently. Do not expect the communications function to do all the work.

---

9   Oliver Engert, Becky Kaetzler, Kameron Kordestani, and Anish Koshy, "Communications in mergers: The glue that holds everything together," McKinsey & Company. https://www.mckinsey.com/business-functions/organization/our-insights/communications-in-mergers-the-glue-that-holds-everything-together#:~:text=Communications%20in%20mergers%3A%20The%20glue%20that%20holds%20everything%20together&text=Structured%20communications%20are%20vital%20to,success%20for%20newly%20combined%20organizations.

- Stay up to date. Keep the integration management office, the deal team, and major work streams connected, so that information is up to date and communications are as proactive and effective as possible.

- Be responsive. Collect and respond to feedback regularly and quickly.

RESPOND TO CHALLENGES

You're going to have some ups and downs in any acquisition, regardless of how well thought-out it is. If you think everything is going to be perfect from the first day, you are likely to be thrown off your game if your largest client leaves or a product flaw rears its ugly head, or any number of other unforeseen things happen. The key is to deal with the challenges quickly. You might not have all the information you would like, but decisions need to be made. Taking the long view will help you see your way through the challenges because you know that even if something isn't perfect now, you have time to correct it.

I once had an acquisition where two weeks in the head of finance at the selling company quit. He knew we would probably not need two CFOs, and so he had been looking for another job well before the deal closed. That type of high-level departure is not going to scuttle the entire deal, but it does make it harder to integrate finances and have the institutional knowledge that is often so important when determining why things are done a certain way. His departure was not unexpected—most CFOs know they are going to be let go because you only need one and that is likely to be the one at the buying company—but the timing could have been better.

Earlier in the book, I told the story of the CEO who walked out the door after announcing the sale of the company. That one had a much greater impact than the fleeing CFO, but even then it worked out in the long run. It took a couple of years to sort out because our leadership style was different from what the team had been used to and we had to earn their trust. But we had always considered this a long-term acquisition, and so we had no trouble putting in the time that was needed.

In the same way, take the long view when it comes to the economics of the deal. These things don't pay for themselves in a month or a year. They take several years to pay out. Knowing that will make the inevitable challenges easier to navigate.

People make the company. There is no greater truism in business than that. Professional services firms, in particular, present a distinctive leadership challenge when it comes to merging multiple teams. In professional services firms, the key value-creating resources (technical knowledge and client relationships) are often proprietary to individuals, who may enjoy considerable operational autonomy within their firm. The challenge for senior leaders is to persuade professional staff to remain with the firm and to share these resources with their merger partner colleagues.

How you combine the leadership and staff of two separate entities will significantly impact the deal. Compromises involving staff reorganizations and even reductions in force are often necessary. If both parties have similar organizations, there is a high likelihood of redundant roles. If staff reductions are planned as a result of the transaction, plan to move forward quickly after the signing of the agreements. It is up to the new leaders of the combined firm to authentically use the new values, vision, and mission of the firm to inspire and excite their teams, even in the face of possible change.

Decisions on which employees will be left behind, so to speak, are extremely difficult. The purpose and values that the new firm expects to have will be tested and exposed during these challenges. If redundancies are involved, take the time to identify the employees involved who are most enthusiastic about the merger. Share the vision and mission of the combined firm clearly with them. The individuals whose personal values are more clearly aligned with the new organization will likely step forward too.

Although the leadership of the two companies will want to work together to decide the new structure, sometimes compromising isn't the best way forward, and it will be up to the CEO of the acquiring firm to make the final decision. For example, the head of a company we were buying assured me that his sales director was outstanding. He went on and on about how much of a people person the sales director was and how he would be a perfect fit for the new organization. After the deal closed, it only took about two months for us to realize the director could talk a good game but didn't have the requisite skills to run a sixty-five-person office. He could make you believe that there were all these great things happening, but in reality he couldn't drive the kind of profit we expected. He didn't have a handle on his numbers. All the stuff that I value in my sales leaders he couldn't do. And all the stuff that I don't value in my sales leaders he could do. As soon as we realized that we had made a mistake, we moved to hire someone else who was a better fit for the position.

It's not unusual to make this type of mistake; realize it's not the end of the world. You simply have to correct it as quickly and as thoughtfully as possible.

One of the challenges that needs to be taken care of early, and often isn't, is deciding exactly how much integration you can and need to do. If you are acquiring a company that is similar to yours, with a tangible product line, a full integration makes sense. But if you are adding on ancillary or creative capabilities, you might need to look at things differently. For example, I've mentioned how Investis acquired ZOG Digital and Vertical Measures and rebranded all three as a single entity. That worked well because the product lines were compatible and in the same digital space. However, I've also acquired creative agencies. Making sure we created lasting value with those acquisitions took an entirely different approach.

Instead of integrating the creative agencies into the parent company, we created a stand-alone holding company, similar to Omnicom Group or WPP Group. The culture in creative companies is all about the people. There is no intellectual property per se. No hard assets. You are buying smart people with good ideas. If you lose the chief creative officer, you are basically destroying the company. So, you have to be very careful not to tip the balance. You don't want to get heavy-handed with the integration. You don't want to force a name change or require new processes. That doesn't work in those types of environments. The best way to work with these types of acquisitions is to leave them to do what they do best in their environment. The holding company allows an arm's length acquisition process that lets the acquiring company repatriate profits from multiple agencies while letting each agency continue to do its own thing. There is no doubt that this structure is inefficient from a cost standpoint, but it is often the only way to acquire the creative company or other attractive acquisition that doesn't quite fit into the parent company mold. The holding companies are good at this. As the CEO of one holding company put it to me, "The agency is the brand, not us here at the holding company."

KEY TAKEAWAY

Closing an acquisition is just the beginning. The hard part is to integrate two organizations, to achieve the goals set in the business plan to create lasting value. This is where leadership will make all the difference between success and failure.

In the next chapter, we'll talk about why it is so important for leaders and firms to stand for something, so that stakeholders can align around a shared cause.

CASE STUDY

Yahoo acquires Tumblr

Deal Size: $1.1 billion

Goal: Increase ad revenue by 20 percent

Outcome: Three years later Yahoo ended up writing down the entire acquisition

In May 2013 Yahoo paid $1.1 billion for Tumblr, a blogging and social networking company. At the time Tumblr was one of the most successful online companies in the world. It hosted more than 108 million blogs, had 300 million unique visitors a month and views of 900 posts per second. Yahoo projected that accessing Tumblr's audience would increase Yahoo's views by 50 percent, as well as drive a 20 percent increase in ad revenue. Three years later the web company wrote off the entire purchase price. How did things go wrong so quickly?

Yahoo expected Tumbler to be a huge moneymaker because the web company thought it could tap into Tumblr's primarily millennial user base. But Tumblr was never designed to be an ad generator. In fact, its founder, David Karp, had always actively opposed advertising on the site. With this antiadvertising foundation and culture, it was hard (turned out to be impossible) for anyone to find a way to turn Tumblr's large user base into ad dollars.

This was really the crux of the problem Yahoo had with Tumblr, and should have foreseen. Yahoo was a public company with shareholders who expected a return on their investment. Tumblr was a young digital company with a young creative audience and culture. It was used to doing things its own way and wanted to continue to focus on the user and creative products. Making money was not a core value. This was not a match made in heaven.

Despite the culture clash around advertising, both companies settled into an uneasy alliance until 2015, when the Tumblr sales force was brought under the Yahoo umbrella and moved from Tumblr's headquarters in the Flatiron district to the Yahoo office in Times Square. At the same time, the group was given a $100 million ad sales target. That was pretty much Yahoo throwing down the gauntlet and declaring, "You will make money or else."

The power play pushed out Tumbler's global head of brand partnerships and was the beginning of a sales exodus at the company.

A year later Yahoo began rolling back the sales integration when Tumblr failed to hit its revenue numbers, but it was too late. Media buyers had a hard time making a case to put Tumblr in their media mix when they didn't know when the next reorganization would hit or what the future held for Yahoo.

Yahoo and Tumblr were also behind the curve on ad innovation. Yahoo did not care about the customer experience and had no way to target ads. So, a teenager might see an insurance ad targeted for retirees, or a corporate exec might be pushed ads aimed at first-time homebuyers.

Finally, users began to leave Tumblr because they didn't trust that Yahoo would or could control content safety on the platform. Yahoo was gaining the reputation as the refuge for spammers, and users did not want to be associated with it.

In 2016 Yahoo wrote down $712 million of Tumblr's value. Yahoo and Tumblr were acquired by Verizon in 2017. In 2019 Verizon sold Tumblr to Automatic, reportedly for less than $3 million.

SUCCESS OR FAILURE?

All in all Yahoo did not know what it was buying and had no idea what to do with Tumblr once it had it. The execs at Yahoo saw a huge user base and thought it would translate into ad revenue. Tumblr execs saw a public company that put money over people. Neither understood the other, and it was only a matter of time before things fell apart—though being part of the internet age, the decline occurred at digital speed.

CHAPTER EIGHT

STAND FOR SOMETHING

n the previous chapter, I outlined how I worked with the board of Investis to change its strategic focus and move the company's strategy in a completely different direction. What I didn't mention was the challenge it presented and how long it would take. I was hired to reinvigorate the company and drive growth. The board knew I would shake things up a bit, but they were envisioning something along the lines of the rumble you get when a train passes by. Instead, I presented them with a 7.0 earthquake–type shake up.

When I arrived on the scene, it was obvious something had to change. If a company is gaining sales at reduced margins and growth has slowed to a single-digit pace, the marketplace is telling you that it is not interested in what you have to sell. It didn't take long to realize that over the years, Investis had slowly evolved into a different company. It was no longer an investor relations or communications company—it was a digital content company. If it was going to grow, it needed to embrace what it actually was and market itself to customers who wanted what Investis had to offer. On top of that, Investis needed to add capabilities such as SEO to its product suite, and the quickest and most efficient way to do that was through acquisition.

All of this meant I needed to go to the board and tell them we had to change our focus from what we had always focused on and move in a new direction. I wasn't going to magically come up with innovative ways to drive profits for an investor relations company that, from my perspective, was really a digital content company. Instead, I wanted to rebrand the company as a digital communications company and spend significant capital to acquire additional capability that could help us expand our capabilities as we looked to build a digital communications hub in future years. I had to be careful with how I presented my proposal. I believed the future of the company depended on the board understanding what needed to be done and committing to doing it. We all know how annoying it can be for a new teammate or employee to tell you that the direction you have been taking needs to change.

The next time the board met, I was ready. I articulated the vision that put Investis in the digital content business and explained why we needed to rebrand in order to realign our communications and customer outreach with that reality. It would have been very easy, especially for the people in London, to discount everything I said. "What does he know? He's never worked in the investor relations / communications industry." And yet they didn't.

After several meetings, the board and senior leaders came around to my way of thinking. They were willing to give the new strategy direction a chance. And just as importantly, they were willing to acquire the companies we needed to exponentially increase our capabilities. It's not cheap for one company to acquire another. This was quite a risk for a company struggling to increase revenues and meet growth projections.

The board accepted my plan because they could see I was committed. Despite the fact that I was relatively new to the company and the industry, I was a digital marketing veteran and focused on making the necessary changes to succeed. I was willing to stand behind my proposals, and the board respected that. Standing for something is an important element of any M&A.

WHY STAND FOR SOMETHING?

In this day and age, firms need to stand for something as much as people need to stand for something. Employees have many choices when it comes to whom they want to work for. Customers have many choices when it comes to whom they want to work with. And attractive companies often have more than one suitor and thus can afford to be choosy on whose advances they want to accept.

Being a firm that is known for its values—whether they focus on customer service, innovation, social activism, the company's shared values, creativity, or any number of other value-based aspects—will often set you apart from others that simply all blur together because there is nothing that differentiates one from another.

In addition, and maybe most importantly, being a firm that is known for standing behind its values will almost always give you an advantage in acquisition negotiations. I can't tell you how many times I've had the CEO of the company I've been interested in acquiring tell me, "Don, you weren't the highest bidder, but I know where you stand on the things that are important to me, and I trust that you'll stand behind all you believe in and honor your word and your promises. We look forward to being part of your organization."

While I like to think that most values are relatively neutral in a corporate setting—companies with top-down leadership are as successful as those with bottom-up structures, companies with rigid processes are as successful as those with more flexible processes, and collaborative companies are as successful as siloed companies—I also know that employees and staff will not follow a leader who doesn't stand for the things they find important.

But when they trust the leader, they will follow them anywhere. One of the more well-known stories of leadership involves Ernest Shackleton's quest to reach the South Pole in the early 1900s. He had two failures under his belt when he began planning a third try in 1914. The story goes that he advertised for crew members by placing a newspaper ad that read:

> *Men wanted for hazardous journey. Low wages, bitter*
> *cold, long hours of complete darkness. Safe return doubtful.*
> *Honor and recognition in the event of success.*

You wouldn't think this type of ad would have many takers, but Shackleton is said to have received five thousand applications. To make his decision easier, he sorted them into piles: nutcases who wanted to do something strange, the hopeless with nothing else going on in their lives, those with potential, and so on. He eventually narrowed the field down to twenty-seven crew members for his newest attempt to reach the South Pole. This trip, too, would prove to be a failure. However, no one died, despite the boat getting stuck in ice and the crew being marooned on Elephant Island until help arrived. That was considered a win.

When you step back and analyze why this help wanted ad worked so well, it's not as surprising as it might look at first glance. People like to know what they are getting into. Shackleton's ad painted a rather dire picture of the job—but it was obviously an honest picture. There would be no surprises. This is exactly what employees, customers, vendors, and acquisitions want. They need to know what you stand for because no one likes surprises. If Shackleton could be this honest in an ad, it was a good bet he would be a straight shooter when it came to leading his crew.

Business leaders who communicate clearly about what they stand for generate that same type of loyalty. For example, I have worked for several companies. I am often brought in to help a company regain its former glory or get it on the right path for growth. When that happens, I know I can call on some of the people I've worked with in the past. I don't sugarcoat things. I let them know what we would be dealing with. "I have another challenging company. The performance has gone off the cliff. The pay is below what you are worth. The options aren't that great. It will take us at least three years to turn this thing around, and even then we might not be able to make it happen. When can you start?"

And they all come.

They know who I am. I'm the same guy at the new company as I was at the old. They trust me, and I trust them. My chief operating officer has worked with me for twenty years. My chief technology officer has been with me for twenty years. My head of marketing has been with me for ten years. My HR person has been with me for ten years. I could go on. The advantage of working with people who work well together is that it makes for a much more efficient company. If I am putting in the time to find and vet an acquisition target or integrate one that we've acquired, I need to be able to rely on those leading the day-to-day activities of the company to do it in a way that matches the things I value. And after so many years of working together, they know I am consistent. They know what I stand for, so they can easily get on board.

Now, there will always be people who would like to do things differently, and that's OK. People can have a view of what they want to do, as long as at the end of the day, they are willing to follow the CEO's lead. The CEO is on the hook to create the strategy for the company and to make sure it's headed in the right direction. In the end people have to get on board with it. If someone decides they can't get on board with what the company is trying to do, they will need to move on. I've even done that myself. In the Agency.com case study outlined in this chapter, I note that it became clear that I couldn't support the strategy being implemented by the leadership team. Divisiveness within a company can harm a firm more than any economic shock, and it would do nobody any good if I couldn't give 100 percent of my support to the new strategy. It was obviously time to move on when I could no longer stand for what the company was standing for.

WHEN YOU STAND FOR SOMETHING, OTHERS WILL STAND WITH YOU

I've been in this business more than thirty years, and I've had people follow me to several different companies because they like my style. They relate to the things I believe in and value. There's an openness about it. The main thing about leadership in today's world is consistency. You have to be consistent in your approach every day.

You can't come in one day and be everybody's best friend and then the next day come in and be a jerk to everybody. Then people aren't going to understand who you are or what you stand for, and they're not going to know what to expect when they come to work. But if you come in every day and they know exactly who you are, they will find it easier to trust you.

When I took the reins at Investis US, the company had a flexible, free-spirited culture that encouraged innovation, interaction, and team bonding. This is a typical tech and creative agency culture. However, while this culture suited the business, I soon discovered that it carried over into an evening party culture, which was not so good for business.

> **The main thing about leadership in today's world is consistency. You have to be consistent in your approach every day.**

I don't think of myself as an old fuddy-duddy, but I was uncomfortable with the staff using company-sponsored happy hours to drink and party late into the night, especially when they had to get up the next day and be sharp and ready to give their best to the customers. I set out to gently, yet firmly, change the company culture.

I like having fun, but there are limits. I have had a personal rule throughout my career: no matter what the work event, I never stay past about 10:00 p.m., because nothing positive happens after that hour. Plus, I like my job too much to feel groggy in the morning from staying out late the night before. I didn't want to be the leader in the ivory tower, so I joined in the happy hours, but at the next party, I started saying my goodbyes around 8:30 p.m., and as I headed out the door I said, "Enjoy yourselves, but I look forward to seeing you all bright and early in the morning." Then I left.

This was my approach at all the happy hours: close the tab early—yes, the company was paying—and lead by example. At first, a few people would still step over the line and get a little tipsy or do something inappropriate. The next day I would raise an eyebrow as I heard the gossip. "You should have seen Sam last night. Don't know how he got into work today!" Well, you can bet I'm going to walk by and ask Sam how he is feeling. If you do that enough, Sam gets the idea that his behavior is being noticed—and not in a good way.

It wasn't long before a happy hour event was wrapping up at 9:00 p.m., and someone said, "Time to go. Right, Don?" I left the restaurant pleased that my consistent actions had been noticed. Little by little the party atmosphere slowed down, and now it's in line with the overall culture being cultivated at the firm.

When your leadership team and employees operate from the same values, they are implicitly in agreement on the culture and you will have a far easier time getting buy-in across the organization. Culture is memetic; when one or two employees emulate your behavior, other employees will emulate them and the culture will pervade the entire organization. An organization that has a cohesive culture isn't distracted by petty disagreements. Employees with a shared culture work together toward a common defined purpose, which has a direct impact on your profit.

Consistency is also crucial to finding and integrating successful acquisition targets. If you don't handle every acquisition with the same amount of integrity, word spreads. If you take advantage of somebody on one deal, people are going to hear about it. Then, when you approach an attractive company, they are going to reject your overtures, or at least make the vetting process difficult, because they've heard that you're not a good guy to work with. The opposite is just as true. If you are consistent in your approach and stand behind your promises, companies will be eager to work with you. We have often acquired firms for less than others offered simply because the founders or leadership team preferred to be part of our organization. So, every deal has to be handled with integrity. It pays dividends in the end.

COMMUNICATE, COMMUNICATE, AND COMMUNICATE SOME MORE

An organization's culture lives and dies with the visionary leader—the CEO influences the culture within the organization by articulating and embedding values, hiring and growing talent, and aligning organizational systems. The leader's values define and drive the organization's culture. So own it. Our job as leaders is to consistently live our values because they create a framework for everyone—internal and external—to connect to. If you're not behaving in a way that reflects your values, no one else will either.

Your leadership team, employees, clients, and partners all need to know what you stand for and why. The saying "Actions speak louder than words" could not be truer when it comes to demonstrating the values that you want to instill in your culture.

Leaders must tell people what they stand for and lead by example. Align your words and actions, which demonstrates that you mean what you say and say what you mean. Reinforce shared values in the company culture is a combination of communication and team-building exercises. Communicate, and do it frequently!

You probably already communicate with your team members in various ways, such as through email or performance reviews. But those traditional ways do not provide enough opportunities for employees to truly open up and completely buy into the culture. Take advantage of current trends and opportunities to host town hall meetings or develop an in-house podcast. Use Slack or other in-house message systems. Share successes and point out how those successes were made possible because of the values you all share—don't assume everyone will just intuit that standing strong on your values will result in success.

Being consistent in what you stand for and relentlessly communicating the company's values are even more important when you are trying to integrate a recently acquired firm. When values flow from the founder and develop organically as a company grows, it is easy for everyone to know what they are. It is not so easy, however, when a buying firm is working to bring the selling firm into the fold.

Investis Digital is the result of integrating three companies in recent years—Investis, ZOG Digital, and Vertical Measures. Since I was the CEO of Investis US and the leader of the acquiring firm, it was always going to be the Investis culture that dominated. That meant we had to integrate the employees and staff of the acquired firms into the Investis culture while recognizing that they might have values that would enrich ours. We had C-level meetings to define our shared values. We had staff- and employee-level team bonding activities that reinforced the values. And we set up communications channels that reiterated them daily. We ended up with a very smooth transition because everyone was able to be part of promulgating the final shared values list.

This openness to listen and look for solutions is a value in and of itself. For example, we have a music server that pipes music throughout the office. All employees are encouraged to add songs they like to the playlist. One woman loaded the playlist with songs from the seventies, dominating the space with her music choices. Others in the office started to complain that they wanted to hear different genres. Rather than turn the situation into a human resources issue, we had everyone participate in an office-wide project. We set a limit to the number of songs any one person could contribute but encouraged everyone to post their favorites. The playlist ended up being quite diverse, and no single genre or time period dominated. We also recognized that not everyone would want to listen to every kind of music, so we purchased headphones for anyone who didn't want to listen to the office music. Those using the headphones could listen to their personal music choice—or no music at all. Only six people opted for headphones. The others were happy with the company playlist because they all felt part of creating it.

SHARED VALUES

Having shared values that everyone understands not only makes it easier for the company to move forward, but it also makes it easier to survive hard times. When hard decisions need to be made, employees and clients understand that those decisions are based on something. They aren't capricious. If personnel cuts need to be made, knowing that it really isn't personal can help lessen the sting.

I was at Agency.com during the dot-com crash around 2000, and we were losing business left and right. To save the company, we had to cut costs, which meant we had to significantly reduce our workforce. You need to stand up and do the hard things in person, so I was spending days telling one person after another that they were no longer employed by Agency.com. Eventually, I left Agency.com and went to iCrossing. This was at the beginning of the financial crash in 2008, when the markets went south again. Just as I had done eight years earlier, I had to tell people they were no longer part of the company. One day I was delivering the news to some of our people in New York. I'm going down my list, and I call this one fellow into my office. He knows why I'm there, and he says, "I don't know if you remember this or not, but this is the second time you've let me go. You let me go at Agency.com, and I joined iCrossing. Now you're letting me go again. Do me a favor; I like you a lot, but please don't ever come to work at the same place I am again."

No one wants to be let go, but when they know that you are being straight with them, they can handle the disappointment with grace—and sometimes humor.

Being firm and transparent in what you stand for also helps when you have to make a decision that not everyone agrees with. For example, when iCrossing acquired Proxicom, I was told that I would want to take care of the company's current leader. My board really liked him and wanted me to give him anything he wanted to make sure he stayed. So, I set up a meeting to see what sort of role he wanted to take now that iCrossing was integrating his firm.

"I know exactly the job I want," he said.

"What is that?"

"I want your job," he said in all seriousness.

"Well, last time I checked, my job was taken. But you're more than welcome to go talk to my board and determine for yourself if that job is taken."

And that's exactly what he did. He was so sure of himself that he went to the board and told them the only job he wanted was my job. At our next meeting, I asked him how his board meeting had gone.

"They say that job is taken and you're the guy who has it."

"And that's the only job you want?" I asked.

"That's the only job I want."

"OK. Then it's been good working with you."

I let him go. And that was the best decision I ever made. He was high performing but also high maintenance. It's often hard to let those types of people go because you can see clients walking out the door with them, but if you don't give them everything, if you don't coddle them, then they will undermine you every time they can. They don't believe they need to be part of the team, and they can pull the entire company down.

If you consistently stand for something, you will have the support of your board, your employees, your vendors, and everyone else you work with. That's a pretty good way to lay a foundation for success.

It's hard for a founder to sell his or her firm. They've put their life into making a dream a reality. They don't want to see it absorbed without a second look or, worse, treated badly by the new owner. Every attractive company has more than one potential buyer. If you have made a career of standing for something, being authentic, and following through on your commitments, you will stand a much better chance of acquiring the firms you need to boost your firm's growth. Who wouldn't want to be part of a firm like that?

KEY TAKEAWAY

There was a time when growing the bottom line was all that counted. If you did that, you were a success. That time is long gone. Today's employees and customers want to know that the companies they work for and do business with stand for something more. They want to be part of a company whose values align with theirs. Being transparent in what is important to your company and what it stands for will put you in good stead when you look to acquire a company.

CASE STUDY

Omnicom acquires Agency.com

Purpose: Expand Omnicom's digital capabilities

Outcome: By 2010 the Agency.com name had disappeared in the US; it disappeared in Europe the following year

My tenure at Agency.com was a time that illustrated just how important compatible shared values are to a successful integration, as well as how standing up for something doesn't mean you will always win. Sometimes you need to recognize when your stand is going nowhere and you need to retreat so you can go on to stand again.

Agency.com was one of several small but growing digital agencies that Omnicom acquired in the late 1990s, just as digital marketing was moving into the mainstream. However, the dot-com bust hit Agency.com as hard as it hit other digital firms, and I was hired to help it recapture its former glory. I was able to turn it around by focusing on customer needs and bottom-line accountability. By 2005 Agency.com was winning multiple awards for its creative work and had grown to be the fourth largest interactive digital agency in the country. My goal was to continue to grow Agency.com as a stand-alone entity under the Omnicom umbrella.

Omnicom had other ideas.

When Omnicom began to acquire digital agencies, it kept them separate from its traditional shops. Digital marketing was a very small part of a client's spend, and the leadership, web-centric culture, and infrastructure were so different from traditional agencies that it made sense to allow these newcomers to remain semiautonomous. But as clients began increasing ad spends for campaigns with a digital focus,

Omnicom decided that rolling their digital holdings into their traditional advertising networks made sense. And on paper it did. But in real life, the clash of cultures was a sticking point from the beginning.

Agency.com was moved to Omnicom's TBWA Worldwide subsidiary in 2005, with an edict from the top to integrate. One of the main problems with integration was that the TBWA management team did not understand Agency.com. In my first presentation to them, I was describing what we did, and I mentioned our "search" capability. One of the top TBWA execs from Europe interrupted me and asked me what we were searching for. I told him search was SEO in this case. His face went to the next level of puzzlement. I had to back up all the way to the beginning and start with an overview of what digital marketing is and what it hopes to achieve. It was a completely foreign concept in an advertising world that revolved around the thirty-second TV spot. Our language and metrics were different (e.g., length of engagement, number of clicks, number of pass-throughs, etc.), as were our channels. If your bosses have no idea what you do—and not a soul at TBWA knew what we did for a living—it is hard for them to lead.

This lack of knowledge did not give anyone at Omnicom or TBWA pause, and the integration process continued. The integration started with the dismantling of the Agency.com network of offices. Agency.com local offices were consolidated into TBWA local offices. Creatives who were used to being autonomous were now reporting to middle managers who had no experience or understanding of digital marketing. C-level Agency.com execs were reporting to managers at TBWA with zero digital experience. Employees who were used to working in the flexible, casual atmosphere of a digital shop were now expected to conform to the more button-down environment of a traditional advertising agency.

I tried to push back on the integration. Although I understood why corporate would want to combine digital and traditional capabilities in one shop, I didn't believe it was in the best interests of Agency.com. When it became obvious that Omnicom and TBWA were intent on integrating Agency.com, I had no choice but to move on. I was not the only employee to make that choice.

After I left, many other seasoned digital executives left, some even following me to iCrossing. At least a half dozen major clients also defected, including Visa, Miller Brewing, CNN.com, and Discovery Communications. Agency.com's founder and chairman, Chan Suh, was brought back, along with an inexperienced executive named David Eastman, to handle day-to-day operations, but the disruption and chaos at Agency.com put it at a disadvantage when competing with a slew of new, successful agencies in the market.

SUCCESS OR FAILURE?

In 2010 Omnicom dismantled Agency.com in the US market. By the following year, it was essentially defunct in Europe as well, and Chan Suh and David Eastman were nowhere to be found.

At one time Agency.com was one of the largest digital agencies in the world. It took less than fifteen years for poor leadership decisions to drive it totally out of business, brand and all.

CHAPTER NINE

THE VALUES COMPATIBILITY PROFILE

At my first job, I remember seeing a laminated "We Stand For" statement hanging on the wall in a rarely used room, but no one ever talked about those values that we supposedly stood for. In fact, I'd guess that only two or three people in the company even realized we had such a statement. Our one and only goal was to make a profit. Talking about the values that supported the company culture was probably seen as a waste of time by the executive team—if they even thought of them at all. Luckily, times have changed.

If you've read this far in the book, you now undoubtedly understand how important it is to have a set of corporate values that everyone in the company can rely on and how crucial it is to take those values into consideration during the acquisition process. Competing values systems really can—and often do—make the difference between success and failure. But knowing that you need to take values compatibility into account and knowing how to effectively do it are two different things.

As I outlined in the first chapter, we have long known that values are important in the merger and acquisition world. Yet despite studies dating back to the 1980s, which consistently proved that values played a significant role in the success and failure of acquisitions, we still don't have a set of standards or metrics that everyone can use to determine if the values of a target company are compatible with those of the acquiring company.

They say the hardest step in solving a problem is admitting you have a problem to begin with. There is no doubt that the industry has admitted it has a problem. So, in this case, taking that first step wasn't so hard. But after more than forty years of admitting we have a problem, we still haven't come up with a viable solution.

That means each CEO or head of corporate development ends up evaluating values in ways unique to their own personality and experience. And that can cause problems. Does the CEO really have a firm grasp of their own company's values and culture? Can they objectively evaluate the acquisition company's values, given that the CEO of that firm might not be able to objectively articulate their own values? Can they look at a value set and predict which ones will work in an integrated entity and which ones will need to change?

Even if a company is able to accurately list its own values, as well as those of the selling company, it needs to know what each value set portends for the future combined company. Does having both companies focused on collaboration signal a successful acquisition? Does having one company focused on innovation and another focused on long-term growth signal failure? Does it matter if one company's entire identity is based on a customer-first culture and the other company is fine treating customers well but is more committed to keeping an eye on costs? How closely do the values need to align? Is it OK if they are different as long as an integration plan takes those differences into account? So many questions. So few answers.

If answering these questions is so important, why haven't we found a universally accepted solution before now? I'd posit it is because values are soft. They aren't the type of things that a CEO or finance and legal team typically deals with. Management teams are happy to give lip service to the importance of values in an M&A transaction, but in their heart of hearts, most executives really don't place values on the same level as the hard data aspects of an acquisition.

In addition, most companies don't get involved in lots of acquisition deals. That means the management team never really gets the experience needed to intuitively assess the values of the acquired firm. Conversely, the firm being acquired has likely never been part of an acquisition before, so its management team would be unaware of what it needs to look for in a perfect transaction.

We also have human nature to contend with. When a CEO or acquisitions team is excited about acquiring another firm and wants to make the deal work—or when the founder of a selling firm is anxious to cash out and move on—it is human nature to minimize or willfully ignore red flags. We tend to view any obstacle to what we want to accomplish as just temporary or something we can work out later. To keep emotions and rose-colored glasses out of deal making, the M&A world has developed standardized checklists that cover all aspects of financial and legal due diligence and help us keep our decision-making focused on objective data rather than wishful thinking. Unfortunately, we don't have that type of template for values due diligence.

Instead, everyone reinvents the wheel the first time they become involved with a merger or acquisition. I happen to enjoy sitting down with my counterpart and getting to know them. Over the years I've figured out what questions I need to ask to get to the heart of their company values and culture. I like to think I've gotten pretty good at knowing when a company's values will be compatible with mine. But I gained that insight through experience. No one has that experience when they lead their first acquisition deal. And not everyone enjoys the personal interaction that getting to the heart of a company's values requires. As a result, a lot of good prospects fall apart because of that lack of experience and lack of an objective values survey.

It seems obvious that we need to develop a standardized values survey template, or a Values Compatibility Profile (VCP), that everyone can use, the same way they use financial and legal checklists.

So, what to do? Well, it seems obvious that we need to develop a standardized values survey template, or a Values Compatibility Profile (VCP), that everyone can use, the same way they use financial and legal checklists. The purpose of a VCP model would be to determine the degree of value alignment for each of the merging parties during the transaction's preclose "diligence" phase. That means it needs to be more than a simple checklist of values. It needs to be an assessment that results in *meaningful* data. In other words, we need a way to predict how the mixing and matching of specific values will affect the performance of a postclose acquisition.

Until we have that tool, those involved in mergers and acquisitions will continue to struggle to assess values and many will simply not do so at all.

HOW CLOSE ARE WE?

The reason we don't yet have a standardized tool is because building one is hard. It takes time, energy, and skills that most managers don't have, even if they were interested in doing it. Acquisitions simply aren't top of mind for most managers. There just aren't enough of them to merit everyone's attention.

However, being a minor function of the market doesn't mean it's a waste of time to make M&A deals better. And hard doesn't mean impossible. If we start at the beginning and rationally work our way to the end, it should be very doable to develop a values due diligence tool that will significantly reduce the number of transactions that fail because values were misaligned.

So, let's start at the beginning. The first thing we need to do is think about what it would look like. From my years of experience, it would seem clear that a workable VCP needs to be:

- Easy to use—no one will add a piece to their already complicated due diligence if it is too time consuming or hard to implement.

- Objective—the results should be based on measurable metrics supported by empirical evidence rather than gut feel.

- Standardized—if there are too many variables and undefined definitions, the conclusions will be inconclusive.

- Predictive—the entire goal is to predict whether or not the values of two companies are compatible.

Now, where do we stand on developing a VCP that meets these four objectives? We're closer than you might think because we have a lot of the foundational work already done. We still need to take the information we currently have and determine the gaps, fill those gaps, and develop the VCP form—but we are moving in that direction.

CURRENT RESEARCH

We already have people out there doing research that—with a few tweaks—a meaningful values assessment could be based on. To date, this research has primarily examined dimensions of a single culture, not the dynamics of compatibility between two merging cultures. In addition, those who claim to be looking at compatible values are often actually looking at strategic fit. Strategic fit is broadly characterized as the similarity between or complementary nature of two companies' strategies. The idea is that if the strategies are similar, the integration will be relatively easy and both companies will benefit from the other's skills and experience. It might seem intuitive to conclude that strategic fit plays an essential role in a merger's or acquisition's financial success, but objective research proves otherwise. According to researchers,[10] acquisitions of companies with complementary strategies typically do not fare any better than acquisitions of companies with differing strategies.

So, this research doesn't quite get us to where we need to be, but it moves us closer, if only by showing us the direction we don't want to take.

It appears that it is not the strategy that is most important—though you wouldn't want to completely ignore a poor fit. It is the values underlying the company's culture that are the deciding factor on

---

10   Chatterjee, S., Lubatkin, M.H., Schweiger, D.M., and Weber, Y., 1992. "Cultural differences and shareholder value in related mergers: Linking equity and human capital," *Strategic Management Journal*, 13(5): 319–334.

whether a deal will succeed or struggle. It is not an exaggeration to say how companies handle culture-related matters is probably the single most decisive factor that can make or break a deal. Although cultural integration is of high importance, it is often hard to anticipate, analyze, and quantify. This is why developing a predictive tool is so hard. We *describe* cultural values rather than measure them. And descriptive words always carry more than a bit of nuance and uncertainty.

An additional hurdle in using current research as a foundation for a standardized VCP is that the researchers have not used a standardized metric for success. Some have employed subjective performance assessments obtained from managers involved in the acquisition or external expert informants. Others have relied on objective measures, including the acquirer's stock market returns or profitability gains. Still others have focused on whether the acquired firm is subsequently divested. Without a standardized measure of success, it is difficult to draw a consensus conclusion on which values are important for success.

Despite all of these hurdles, the current research serves the important purpose of helping us define what we are looking for. We know what we have isn't quite right, so what do we need to do differently?

MEASURING UNDERSTOOD VALUES VERSUS ESPOUSED VALUES

As mentioned above, if we are going to develop empirical studies that help us put together a predictive values model, we need to agree on a standardized definition of success. You can't predict success if you don't know what success looks like. In addition, we need to focus on the values underlying culture, not on strategies. Finding metrics to measure values is difficult for many reasons, not the least of which is that culture and the values that underlie it are amorphous. Unlike financials—which can be inputted into a database to be tracked and measured—values can, and often do, unpredictably mutate over time. Initially, the underlying culture and values tend to be significantly influenced by the founder, governance bodies (board of directors), and the key participants who define the organization. Over time, changes in ownership and key executives evolve the culture, making it hard to definitely assess the inconstant values driving it.

Thus the challenge with trying to quantify values is the subjective and complicated nature of cultural measurement. However, we can divide values into two categories—shared and espoused—and begin to pull out the ones that can be quantified.

Shared values are often simply picked up by osmosis in the organization. Employees learn quickly the preferred methods of communication and interaction. Some organizations encourage employees to drop by each other's desks, while others lean toward setting up appointments. Some organizations prefer written communications, while others value face-to-face interaction. Some rely on phone calls, while others choose almost any other method. Coca-Cola was famous for ditching its voicemail function in its Atlanta headquarters because no one listened to them and messages from vendors and clients were going unanswered. Shared values are nearly impossible to quantify because they aren't seen as drivers of the business—they are just how things are done. They tend to define interaction among employees and management rather than drivers of the business.

Espoused values, on the other hand, are a distinct form of organizational values that are increasingly documented and are associated with organizational outcomes. These values might include things such as a focus on innovation, customer service, and commitment to the team. Espoused values are more easily measured and correlated with outcomes than shared values are. Espoused values are deliberately selected and promoted to characterize an organization. At Investis Digital, we held a multiday executive meeting to refine our stated values and then solicited input from both inside and outside the company. It was not a rushed exercise. It was a very purposeful discussion that resulted in the five mission values that drive everything we do.

The trend for organizations to explicitly provide a statement of espoused values now affords us the opportunity to consider this aspect of organizations from a wider empirical perspective. We aren't guessing at what a company stands for; they are telling us. We can begin to build a model that will help us know which values work well together and which don't.

Now that we know the values that we want to quantify— espoused values—we need a way to organize them. One researcher at the University of Bristol, Humphrey Bourne, took this approach by surveying a large number of UK and US companies and collecting their espoused values into a single data set. He then went on to structure those values into a conceptual map that used an analytic process to determine similarity between values.[11]

When analyzing the data, Bourne realized that the values were falling into four areas of emphasis—community, competence, character, and interpersonal. Being able to group values into four emphasis categories lets us begin to build an empirically based picture of how values interact with one another.

So, we now have a background to work with, but we still don't know what it means. Based on Bourne's work, "individuality" falls on the opposite side of the similarity scale from "compliance" and "customers." Does this mean that an acquisition would likely fail if it was trying to match a company that focused on customers with one

---

11   Bourne, H., Jenkins, M. & Parry, E. Mapping Espoused Organizational Values. *J Bus Ethics* 159, 133–148 (2019). https://doi.org/10.1007/s10551-017-3734-9.

that focused on individuality? "Continued improvement" is on the opposite side of the similarity scale from "teamwork." Can't you continually improve through teamwork? Given that a customer-focused company could certainly find common ground with one that values individuality, or a company that valued continued improvement would have no problem also valuing teamwork, the similarity or dissimilarity between values does not in itself seem to be the controlling factor as to whether values are compatible or not. It might be that values on the opposite end of the similarity scale are similar to colors on opposite sides of the color wheel. For example, yellow is on one side of the wheel, while its complementary color, purple, is on the opposite side. We just don't know yet what the location of various values in relation to others means.

This construct is a good step forward in our quest to develop a standardized values assessment, but we still have a long way to go. Taking the next step will involve devising research that looks at a large universe of past M&As and analyzes the values each company brought to the transaction. We can then overlay those values on the Bourne values construct and begin to build a correlation model that helps us predict which values groupings promote success and which suggest a poorer outcome.

HOW TO MAKE IT WORK TODAY

We've been talking about the importance of developing a VCP to help stakeholders assess corporate values before a deal is closed and the type of research we still need to do to get there. We don't have that tool yet, but we certainly aren't going to stop the M&A process while we wait. So, how do we avoid the mistakes so many acquisition teams make while we work on a standard values assessment template?

We use what we do know.

First of all, we don't make judgment calls on corporate values. You certainly wouldn't want to become enmeshed with a company that valued taking advantage of customers. And values such as integrity and honesty should be a given in any transaction. Aside from that very low bar, however, corporate values are neutral. A top-down, military-type system is not inherently good or bad. A freewheeling, individual culture is not inherently good or bad. A firm that values getting its product to the market first, even if there are still bugs to work out, probably won't integrate well with a firm that values quality above speed. But neither culture is inherently wrong. So, you are not looking for a specific, preconceived answer. You are looking to understand the buying or selling company better so you can determine if you can work with it. What does the other firm stand for? What does it put a high degree of importance on? Do the values it holds dear match up with yours or, even better, enhance yours? If they don't match, can you envision them at least coexisting?

For example, Investis Digital emphasizes the quality of its products. If we are building a website, it will be the best website possible. Providing the best product and service for our clients is an end in itself. Another company might also build websites, but for them, the website is just a foot in the door. The quality is OK, but they actually want to sell other products. The focus isn't on the customer's needs; it is on their own needs. I would have a hard time acquiring that company because their view of customer services is so different from mine. That doesn't mean their values are wrong. It just means they don't fit with mine.

I want to also note that the importance of compatible values is partly a function of size. A very large firm acquiring a small niche company will probably not be as aware of values as two equally sized firms would be. This is because the large firm would likely absorb the smaller one rather than integrate. Firms risk losing that special something that made the smaller company so attractive to begin with, but it is rare for a large acquirer to change to meet a small acquired company's wants. Large firms sometimes structure the postclose companies so that the smaller firm keeps its autonomy and culture, but you aren't likely to see the larger firm budge on its values. On the other hand, firms of equal size need to be much more aware of their values compatibility because they will both bring a strong personality to the deal.

BUILD YOUR OWN VALUES SURVEY

Even though we don't have a standardized assessment template yet, you can draw up your own values assessment guide that incorporates the things you find important. You can start from scratch or use published versions, such as the one I've included in chapter 4, and tweak it to suit your needs. These surveys all rely on the participants being able to verbalize and describe their values correctly, which isn't a given, but it's a good place to start.

The best way to get better at evaluating acquisitions is to simply get started. As you assess the ones you've done over time, you will learn what works and what to avoid and will be able to adjust your values checklist. Success is based on achieving what you hoped to do to begin with. Did the new technology fill the gap you needed filled? Did you see an increase in market share? Did you increase your revenue gross margin? Whatever you hoped to do, did you do it?

Look for patterns. What characteristic or values did the successful acquisitions bring to the table? What made the integration of less successful acquisitions challenging? Begin to build a personalized values assessment that works for your company.

To make the assessment more viable, try to quantify the values you find important. One way to do this is to assign a set of key performance indicators (KPIs) to each value. The truly soft values such as kindness and respect are hard to quantify, but many others can be measured on how well they meet a KPI. In fact, the values that can be quantified are probably the values that will make or break the deal.

As an example, one of Investis Digital's espoused values is "Keep Innovating." We have metrics that track how innovation is driving growth. We can confidently say that innovation is one of our core values because it is crucial to our success. We measure all of our espoused values to make sure they are truly affecting everything we do. When it comes time to acquire another company, I would be looking to assess their espoused values the same way.

> **When companies do retrospectives on what went wrong with an acquisition, culture is cited as the primary issue time and time again. Yet culture is often initially overlooked among the countless considerations that go into a successful merger or acquisition.**

When companies do retrospectives on what went wrong with an acquisition, culture is cited as the primary issue time and time again. Yet culture is often initially overlooked among the countless considerations that go into a successful merger or acquisition. Leaders frequently emphasize financial and strategic fit alone because these areas are quantifiable and directly tied to monetary gain. Ironically, financial gain isn't possible without cultural compatibility, alignment of values, and a shared vision. Cultural fit is critical; it is the only way to unite teams, achieve shared goals, and create sustainable success.

KEY TAKEAWAY

The keys to assessing values come down to:

- Making your firm's and your target firm's values measurable

- Expanding your due diligence to evaluate their alignment

- Establishing each firm's chief differentiators—the guiding principles that influence their organization's culture and decisions. These are usually immutable and need to be at the forefront of any analysis.

- Analyzing the personalities and processes that make up your culture and comparing them to those of your potential partner

- Using your core beliefs to create a values checklist by which you can determine the merits of the deal from a cultural standpoint

- Determining your compatibility to the best of your ability before you move forward

CASE STUDY

Merger of BBDO Worldwide, Doyle Dane Bernbach, and Needham Harper Worldwide to create Omnico

Deal Size: $40+ million spent in first year to integrate the three companies

Purpose: To harness the creativity of three world-class agencies into one

Result: More than thirty years later, Omnicom is the second largest advertising agency in the world

In 1986 Allen Rosenshine, John Bernbach, and Keith Reinhard cocreated Omnicom in a three-way merger of BBDO Worldwide, Doyle Dane Bernbach (DDB), and Needham Harper Worldwide. Each of these agencies had been around for decades and had been influential in the growth of the US advertising industry. The goal of the merger was to bring together the capabilities of three equals into one massive, worldwide agency.

Initially, the process of combining three competing agencies under one umbrella corporation, Omnicom, raised concerns. More than $40 million was spent on merger- and restructuring-related costs, leaving the company essentially profitless for its first year. Several clients were opposed to the merger and expressed their displeasure by taking their business elsewhere. RJR Nabisco left immediately, with the chairman reportedly declaring that with very few exceptions, the wave of mergers occurring at the time only caused disruption to the clients and only benefited shareholders and managers of the agencies.

By the time the dust had settled after the merger, the three Omnicom agencies had lost $184 million in billings that were directly attributable to the act of the merger itself.

The following year the company acquired several high-profile clients and took in $280 million of new business, but they also lost several significant long-term clients. In 1987 Omnicom earned only $32 million from commissions and fees of $785 million, or 4.1 percent in what traditionally was a double-digit margin business. The merger was not delivering its desired and expected results.

Up to this point, Allen Rosenshine, CEO of BBDO, had been spearheading the integration. This was not what he had signed up to do. He was the CEO of an ad agency, not an M&A expert. With his blessing, the board of Omnicom brought in former BBDO CEO Bruce Crawford to manage the restructuring and become Omnicom's CEO. Crawford moved quickly to streamline the organization, divesting a number of Omnicom businesses and shuttering others. Omnicom was left with a strong core to build from. By the beginning of the 1990s, Crawford's strategy was working. By 1995, when Omnicom recorded an 18 percent increase in revenues to $2.3 billion and a 26 percent gain in net income to $140 million, the company was a force to be reckoned with. Growth continued the following year, when amid the accolades and applause directed at its three subsidiary agency companies, Omnicom posted strong financial totals, registering a 26 percent gain in net income in 1996 to $176.3 million and an increase in revenues from $2.3 billion to $2.64 billion.

At this point Crawford felt he had proven that the holding company could work in the advertising / marketing communications world and Omnicom was on solid ground. He stepped down in 1997 and turned the reins over to John Wren. Today, Wren oversees a holding company with more than 1,500 interconnected communications agencies employing approximately 70,000 people, located in 100-plus countries serving more than 5,000 clients. Revenues for 2019 came in at $15 billion, with an operating profit of $2.2 billion. Wren's record of success over an extended period is unsurpassed.

WHY DID IT WORK?

Merging three extremely successful and longstanding advertising firms into one new marketing communications company could have gone very badly. In fact, the first couple of years made everyone wonder if they had made a mistake. However, the management team working to transform the three agencies into one new company did several things right, as well as having one very important aspect working in their favor.

First of all, they kept their eyes on the long-term prize. They recognized the need for new leadership early and didn't hesitate to bring someone in with the talent, skills, and foresight to restructure the three entities into one. This change allowed each of the original three CEOs to focus on running their own divisions, while someone else could concentrate on the mechanics of running the holding company.

Secondly, the three CEOs were willing to accept the new strategy, which focused on streamlining the business as opposed to trying to mesh all of the original parts.

Finally, everyone recognized the need to allow creative agencies the flexibility to do things their own way. Omnicom's structure was set up to streamline the back-office type functions and provide all the agencies access to a variety of clients (i.e., clients often use multiple agencies under the Omnicom brand), but the day-to-day culture within each agency was left alone. Wren, who has remained CEO of Omnicom for many years, is known to say, "The agencies are the brand, not Omnicom."

The aspect that all three original agencies brought to the table and that made this all possible was shared values. All of the agencies respected the creativity of their employees. All were client-focused. And although they were competitors, they all respected each other's capabilities. Coming from a place of respect for each other's organizations and employees' talents made the bumps in the road annoying but not fatal. Without these shared values, the end result might have been very different.

CONCLUSION

The importance and popularity of mergers and acquisitions as a means of achieving corporate growth and profit objectives are well established. If you are happy with the size and profitability of your company and you just want to be part of the crowd, then "steady as she goes" will probably work for you—though it is hard to continue to be profitable in the long term solely based on organic growth. But if you want to step out from the crowd, you need to look at acquiring other companies.

However, despite the popularity of the "doing the deal" and despite the fact that acquisitions are an efficient way to grow, the evidence is that acquisitions, on average, do not improve the performance of the firms they acquire. While some firms have created a competitive advantage by securing companies at attractive prices and excelling at integration, most companies cannot unlock the synergies and strategic rationale touted as reasons for the acquisition.

To do it right, you need experience, and no one has that experience in the beginning. That is why it is so important to know up front that M&As involve more than financial statements and legal contracts. Successful integrations depend on values compatibility.

Recent statistics show that over 75 percent of mergers and acquisitions fail. In the US only 15 percent achieve their financial objectives, typically measured as shareholder value, return on investment, and performance after merger or acquisition.[12] Among the most frequently cited sources of firm integration problems are culture clashes between the firms. It is not surprising, then, that managers and researchers are increasingly interested in how differences between two organizational cultures impact mergers and acquisitions' outcomes—and how they can predict those impacts preclose.

Successful acquisitions involve many moving parts, whether they are financial, legal, or cultural. I've been involved in many M&As over the years, and I know that they are marathons, not sprints. There is often a honeymoon period when any bumps in the road are smoothed over or simply ignored. As you get down the road, however, you get tired of those bumps and they seem to get bigger and have more of an impact. They begin to make a difference in how well you are able to move forward as an integrated company. I've developed a few strategies to avoid a bumpy road in the first place and make the long game work when you undertake a merger/acquisition.

Build Capabilities That Leverage Your Values

Throughout this book I've stressed how important it is for your brand values to guide every decision you make about an acquisition. The values of your two companies must be aligned if your transaction

---

12   Habek, M., Kroger, F., and Trum, M., 2000. *After the Merger: Seven Rules for Successful Postmerger Integration*, New York, NY: Prentice-Hall/Financial Times.

has any chance of succeeding (and keep in mind, most of them fail). At the one-year mark, you should be moving past the question of "Are our values compatible?" and focusing on how your combined company can create a stronger offering for your clients.

When Investis bought communications firm ZOG Digital, we leveraged our shared values, such as a commitment to innovation, to develop an approach we call "Connected Content." This initiative allows us to help clients craft brand stories that better reach their audiences through content creation. This approach was the payoff of building a stronger company together, and it guides our entire company today.

Build Your Brand from the Inside Out

You can't slap a new logo or name on a business and say you have a new brand. Yes, visual identity and even a new name might be an outcome of your merged company, but they are manifestations of your brand, not the brand itself. You build your brand by first rallying your own people around your mission, vision, and values. From there, you change behaviors.

A relationship with a brand is emotional, and that reality applies to your people as well. Once they begin to feel an emotional connection to your merged company, then they'll start living your brand, whether they're talking about your company on their socials or proposing work to a potential client. You'll know you've succeeded when you see people on the same page behind the scenes, when your client isn't in the room with you.

Keep Your Eye on Performance

How do you know that your transaction will succeed in the long run? The answer is easy: look at the numbers. Yes, this entire book has focused on why your M&A needs to be rooted in values, but that doesn't mean financial performance is less important. Actually, values should *drive* performance. If you've built a business off shared values, the elements of your combined entity should be cross-selling their capabilities seamlessly. That's because when newly merged businesses cross-sell to their clients, they're making a vote of confidence in each other and they're showing trust in each other. You cannot build that confidence and trust unless you have shared values.

Manage Your Deal Appetite

A word of caution: when you pull off a successful acquisition, it's tempting to ask, "What's our next deal in the pipeline?" It's a funny thing about acquisitions: They can become like a fine wine or a gourmet dish. You develop a taste for them, and you want more. Make sure you keep mergers/acquisitions in perspective. They are a means to an end, not an end unto themselves. Always remember: values come before acquisitions.

FINAL WORD

Deals are a legacy of the leader, and whether they fail or succeed often rests on their shoulders. Know that success isn't random. It comes to those who know what it takes to integrate two companies: a due diligence process that gives values compatibility the same level of importance as financial, strategic, product, and legal components, as well as a postclose process that works to integrate the two companies into one with a shared vision. It's not easy but it is oh-so-satisfying. Good luck. And watch for a VCP in the not-too-distant future. It's coming.

DON SCALES

Don has been part of the professional services world for more than three decades. During that time he has led over forty merger and acquisition transactions, primarily on the buying side. He has learned firsthand what works and what doesn't and has long thought about writing a book to share his knowledge with others. *The M&A Solution: A Values-Based Approach to Integrating Companies* is the result of his realization that participants in M&A transactions often fail to focus on one important factor—corporate values.

Don is currently global CEO of Investis Digital, where he is executing on his vision to lead a company unlike anything else in the digital communications space. Through acquisitions, as well as organic growth, he has put together a team with deep expertise in corporate communications and investor relations and united them with innovative performance marketing experts and world-class technology solutions to help companies connect with audiences across all digital touch points.

Don previously led iCrossing from a small search agency to a global full-service digital agency that was acquired by Hearst Corporation for more than $300 million. Prior to that he was CEO of Omnicom Group's Agency.com, where he successfully led the company through a tremendous period of growth. He has also served as managing director of Igate Capital, as well as group vice president of industry consulting of Oracle and senior vice president of management consulting of EDS.

Don has dual undergraduate degrees in chemical engineering and mathematical physics and a master of science degree in chemical engineering from Rice University, as well as an MBA from Harvard Business School. He is currently pursuing his doctorate with a focus on how corporate values impact the long-term outcomes of mergers and acquisitions and the need for a standardized Corporate Values Profile during the due diligence phase.

Outside of work, Don has donated his time the Make-A-Wish Foundation, where he was a member of the North Texas Board of Directors. He also enjoys keeping up with his favorite sports teams with a glass of wine. He is the coauthor, with Fran Biderman-Gross, of *How to Lead a Values-Based Professional Services Firm: 3 Keys to Unlock Purpose and Profit*.